GOD PUT ME UP ON GAME

Kristen R. Harris

Cover Photography: Feel This Moment Photography
Cover Design: German Creative
Editing Services: Faithe Effect

To Auntie Patricia Wells because your spiritual vision is 20/20 and you saw The Book before I could see it.

To Keith because you served as the conduit for the transference of my gift and love of writing.

CONTENTS

ACKNOWLEDGMENTS

Thank you to my entire village because without you, I couldn't do any of what I do. You all are my biggest supporters! So thank you to The Man, my 3 Piece Spicy, my Clutch Girl, my Daddy, my Sissy and my Auntie. Everything I do is to make you all proud!

Welcome To

The GAME

MY MIND EXPLODED, AND THIS BOOK IS THE AFTERMATH

Hey you! I am so delighted that you have decided to join me on these pages. Whether you are reading because the title piqued your interest, or someone recommended it to you or even if you are just trying to be nosey, I am elated! To know that you decided to spend a fraction of your hard-earned wages or dedicate a few moments of your precious time on what I have authored is something that I will never take for granted. Don't worry. We'll get to the formal introductions later, but for now let me try to explain just what you're getting yourself into!

The stories that you will read here are my life experiences that were trapped in my mind as mere memories, which have now spilled across these pages, and supernaturally formed a book! It was composed all over the place: in my phone, in a journal, on my laptop, with voice recordings, via random Facebook posts, on bill envelopes in the car, virtually anywhere inspiration hit me. For that reason, this is not a typical memoir or autobiography told in chronological order and it is worth mentioning how this uncanny literary piece works. Sometimes I will speak directly to you in my voice. Then there will be times where it is not me, but God himself who wants your attention. (Even if you don't know the difference now, by the end you should understand how to differentiate your voice from that of God's.) And honestly, if I leave room for Him to flow through me, my words will be His anyway. You will have a better understanding of that as well by the time you cross that imaginary finish line. Still, there will be other times when I am speaking directly to God or maybe even to myself. Lastly, you may think I am bat crazy when I start talking directly to the person who I am referring to in the story. Please don't start frantically looking around like you are trying to figure out who I am directing my conversation to either. That will only make you seem as bat crazy as me and I am sure that's no fame you care to claim! (Us brown girls love to talk right to a person who is nowhere around! We can narrate a story like no other group of women known to man.)

Oh, yea. Then there's the thing where I deviate from the entire story altogether simply because there is a much more important piece of information that I must share at that precise moment. Oh wait – There's really just one more thing that you need to know as you prepare to dive in and I cannot forget this one. I am a self-certified music head. I might say something that instantly reminds me of a song lyric, so I HAVE to include some of those lines here. This book could probably have an accompanying soundtrack! My play sister says that I have music Tourette's because I will just blurt out music lyrics if I hear one word that triggers my mental music catalog. (Us brown girls love to have play sisters and play cousins too!) See? I did it again.

Look. The point is just flow with me and prayerfully whoever edits this monstrosity will be able to decipher and transform it so that you can comprehend and apply! Mainly, I just need you to focus and pay close attention. Buckle up, keep up, and let's go for a ride! I promise to share all the good game with you.

A LEGEND IS A BORN

November 24, 1980 at 3:35 am – the day that my mother birthed a legend! Kristen Renita Love blessed her family with a creative and tenacious soul. This is probably the moment where you're thinking that I am some narcissistic and egotistical author chick who really has no reason to be so vain. No worries; you are not the first person to conjure up such thoughts! But before you put this book down, please just give me a chance. I promise you this will be well worth any time invested.

Yes, a legend was born when I made my debut on earth. However, I do not refer to myself as a legend because of what I have accomplished in life. It is not about the spectacular things that I have done, though I have done some pretty dope stuff! Nope, I am a legend because truthfully, I should be dead. The circumstances of life have literally tried to kill me, but I am still here. For that reason alone, I am a *living* legend…

SPEAKING OF LEGENDS…

I give all the really important (and a few not *that* important) people and things in my life nicknames. Consider this your legend to understanding who these people are. This is a crash course, so I don't expect you to commit these all to memory. For goodness sake, this isn't an exam; it's just a book!

Just peek back over here if you ever forget.

The Man – My man, my husband
Three Piece Spicy – My daughters (They are not
mentioned in this volume but will make an
appearance in the future.)
Clutch Girl – My mama
Daddy – I'll let you figure that one out
Sissy – My baby sister who isn't a baby anymore
Bestie – My forever friend because she knows too
many secrets
The Biological – Thinking I will leave that one to
you as well
Stanley – My 1st car, a Nissan Stanza
Lil' Money – My 2nd car, a Pontiac Grand Am
Dime Bone – Well, I'll let you meet her later…

KRISTEN RENITA HARRIS, GIRL OF THE SOUTHSIDE

Many will ask why I am sharing all my clean and
dirty truths. My answer is simple. This is MY life.
These are MY experiences. I am telling MY truth.
The experiences God gave me taught me valuable
lessons that I want to share. He allowed me to have
them so that I could eventually empower, inspire
and uplift women just like you. I share (most of) my
life with the world and this is one of the many ways
that God gets the glory out of my life. However,
some people around me can't deal with me being so
raw. I once posted a video of me on social media
where I was in rare form. I was crying and talking
about how hurt I was by women who were tearing

each other down. That was one of those God ideas (we will talk about these later) because I would have never exposed myself like that on my own. There were more than a few people who wanted to know why I shared my vulnerabilities publicly. Many of them were very close to me. They felt like it was too personal or that people didn't need to see me like that. To them, I say, "Don't read this book. You are going to be appalled!" I also say, "If you were ashamed of my struggle days, please don't appear for the plentiful ones." If you have held me down when I was right or when I was wrong, while I have been on this journey, just know I am taking you to the top with me. When I win, you win. When I'm blessed, you're blessed. Greater for me means greater for you. Why? Because while I was in lack, you had my back. When I was down, you stayed around. You already know if you qualify! No explanation needed.

I guarantee that this book is the 100% pure unadulterated truth. However, let me set one thing straight right now. Being the truth simply means that there are no lies in the book. It does not indicate that more truth has not been omitted. My life is an open book, but there are still some chapters that I choose to skip over every now and then. Geesh, stop rolling your eyes. That is my right, you know! Y'all are just nosey anyway! Yes, I said y'all! I am a little brown girl from the Southside of Chicago — which is pretty country if you ask me — who spent the first five years of her formative adulthood in Alabama. So yes, I say — and write — y'all with ease!

There is much inside these pages that I struggled

with writing. However, I had to recall our EmpowerMoments mantra. "When it hurts to WRITE, you've got it RIGHT!" This collection of thousands of words all strung together really pierced me to the core. Yet, I couldn't stop at my tears, so for that reason alone, I know that your life is about to be changed. I not only cried, but I laughed. There were even periods when I stood in awe of my own story! In fact, there are many stories that were only brought to the forefront of my thoughts as I sat down to organize this book. If I have recorded my journey in the most transparent, colorful and personified way, you will feel similar emotions. All I have ever done is tell my story in hopes that whosoever ears it fell upon would be inspired. While penning this memoir, I prayed that God would open your eyes to read the words, open your ears to truly hear my story and open your heart to receive the revelation attached to my highs and lows and I truly believe that He will.

Although everything that I share within these pages is the purest form of truth, most names will never be mentioned. There will be times where an alias is used to protect the person I am speaking of. However, if you already know the story, then you already know the story! Every now and then I may throw a real name out though, but those people won't be anyone looking to sue me. Those are folks who still know and love me. They live in my friend circle and I will throw their names out for validation. These stories that I am telling are true and they can vouch for me! They will tell you exactly what happened and since I am about to blow up from this, they will be excited to tell you that they know me in real life! (I am chuckling, but I am so serious!) My innermost circle has probably heard most of these stories a time or two. My husband, my sister and my best friend know pretty much everything about me. By the time you finish, you will know a lot too. For now, just be cool with knowing that, just like Michelle O., I am Kristen Renita Harris, a girl of the Southside!

Game Is To

Be TOLD

THE GAME IS TO BE TOLD, NOT SOLD

I only have one directive as it pertains to this book -- Anytime you see "**#GPMUOG**" (God Put Me Up On Game), you need to pay very close attention. Embed whatever comes after that string of letters into your mind. If you must, have a pen and pad handy so that you can take copious notes. Or assuming this is your copy to mark up, grab your highlighter and go to work. Those words are important to your life. Say them out loud and repeat them if that's how you remember things because that's some game that God gave me to share with you. And one of the many things that I know about God is that He is not going to send you off.

Let's practice. **#GPMUOG** – If God is saying, "Trust Me," it's going to put you in a better position. Even if you're not in a bad position, wherever He is moving you to is much better. God has game!

Got it? Great, let's get to it!

So, you may be wondering why I entitled this body of work, *God Put Me Up On Game*. The first 'G" may not cause you any uneasiness, but the last one will likely spark a tinge of controversy. The word 'game' has such a negative rep these days, but Game is not a bad thing at all. Many use it for bad purposes, but overall, Game is a great tool to have in your repertoire. Game is essential information to get what you want or need. I am sure you have overheard a friend saying something like, "oh he is spitting game" in response to a man who may be sharing misleading information for the sake of sleeping with a woman he's interested in. I can certainly see how that would taint Game's good name. However, I think he's a smart young man because he fully understands how Game works. He's using the knowledge he has to get what he desires. If you are mad at that, you need to get some Game of your own and you will stop falling for it! OUCH! **#GPMUOG** – Listen to the game that God has for you. It is the essential information required to get what you desire out of this life. God wants to put you up on that good game! After all, His word says that He has plans for you to win. (**Jeremiah 29:11**) You win by knowing the Game!

And they overcame him by the blood of the Lamb and by the word of their testimony. Revelation 12:11 NIV

So, knowing what I do about God, if He gave me this game, it's not just for me. It's to be shared with all women. We must stop being so stingy with information; that's the only way that we can all progress. He made me to empower women and that's exactly what I am going to do. I once had a male friend ask me to stop putting women up on so much game, but I simply cannot honor that request. Truthfully, I almost permanently unfriended him for asking me such ludicrousness. God created me to go through all this stuff, not just for my good but to share my story and help set women across the world free. **#GPMUOG** –When you know your purpose, you will spend every waking moment

11

pursuing that thing until you meet your destiny. Once you meet your destiny, you will dwell there until the day you are called from this earthly realm. This book is a piece of me pursuing that purpose!

THE ORIGIN OF MY GAME

I often hear women praising their fathers for equipping them with all the game they needed to navigate life, love and everything in between. As an official Daddy's girl to my core, it would be safe to assume that my Daddy was the one who schooled me to the game. – *Cooter schooled me to the game, now I know my duty. (Ma$e, Mo Money, Mo Problems)* You just got your first taste of my music Tourette's! – But my Daddy wasn't the source of my game. He protected me, he supported me, and he absolutely provided for me. He picked up where a man who couldn't and wouldn't fulfill his responsibility left me. My Daddy did a heck of a lot for me, even above and beyond what he was never required by law to do. But he was not the one who put me up on game. As a matter of fact, when it came to relationships, I didn't even want my Daddy's game. He was an amazing father, but he was a lousy husband. The only aspects that I took from him were recognizing a hard-working provider and what I wasn't going to accept from a man in a relationship. I haven't decided yet if I'll tell my mama and Daddy's bizarre love story within these pages. But if decide to do so, you will thoroughly understand what I just said.

My husband has taught me a lot about life and

love, so he has certainly contributed to some of the game that I'll share. More on that later. However, it was my Daddy in heaven who made sure I would never lose. He really put me up on major game. Some people would argue that their lessons on game came from the streets. I say that everything we learned in the streets was life experiences and for that reason it's God. He is the one who allowed me to be in those places, have those experiences and most importantly got me out and on to something better. **#GPMUOG** – Even if it wasn't bad where you were, if God moved you it's because where you are is much better than where you were. This is still true, even if it doesn't feel that way. Clearly, He wants you to know that important tidbit of information because it's the second time that I have said it already.

It is vital that you understand that God can share game with you via many different channels. What I will share here is not just from my experiences. We will chat more in-depth about this when we discuss how polite God is to us. He has spoken to me through dreams, friends, social media memes, podcasts, prayers, music, essentially everything. **#GPMUOG** – "You can find Me in everything. I am an omnipresent God."

Now please don't shoot the messenger for what I am about to divulge next. Your greatest game is going to come at some of the hardest and lowest points of your life. That's precisely why you have to embrace your valley seasons. In the depths of your sorrows and pain is where you learn game. When you are struggling with your relationships, finances, employment, or health, you are vulnerable and open to receive the necessary information. Those times when you feel the emptiest are when you find that He limitlessly pours into you. Get that game, girl! You absolutely need it to survive. **#GPMUOG –** Those extremely difficult situations are teaching you great game. Stop running from those circumstances. They are critical to your life success.

Dear brothers and sisters, when troubles of any kind come your way, consider it an opportunity for great joy. For you know that when your faith is tested, your endurance has a chance to grow. So let it grow, for when your endurance is fully developed, you will be perfect and complete, needing nothing. James 1:2-4

THE MOST IMPORTANT GAME IN THIS BOOK

This book is full of that good game that will change your life. However, if you suffer from anything that will make you abandon this book before you complete it, make sure you listen carefully to what I am about to say. Come closer so that you can really hear me. The following two pieces of information are probably the most important in this book and they literally came straight from God to me to you.

#GPMUOG – (1) "Don't worry about pleasing anybody but Me. Stop worrying about what other people think."

God took me through so much to break me of the habit of trying to dance around what people thought of me. There would be times where I wouldn't say or do what God was directing me to because I feared the judgment of people. That line of thinking is ridiculous! I should've been more concerned with the judgment that was coming from above after my continual disobedience. I was also guilty of adjusting who I was so that other people could be comfortable in my presence. I understand that I can be a bit too much for many people and that in essence caused me to dumb and water myself down. **#GPMUOG** – No one wins when you don't show up and be everything that God created you to be. You lose because you are not living up to the fullness of your potential. The recipients of your dumb and watered-down behavior don't win either. No one benefits from you only giving them a piece of who you are. Use everything that God gave you to positively impact the world. Don't ever hold back. Those who are uncomfortable with you being great will either rise to the occasion or they will fall back. The result is growth for them or growth for you. It's a win-win situation when you show up and perform.

For am I now seeking the approval of man, or of God? Or am I trying to please man? If I were still trying to please man, I would not be a servant of Christ. Galatians 1:10 ESV

#GPMUOG – (2) "Always do what I tell you to do. I am not going to send you off. Ever! So, if I tell you to do something, no matter how crazy it sounds, it is because it's what is best for you. Trust Me!" (There it goes again! This obedience thing must be crucial to God.)

This was rather difficult during a particular season of my life because some of the things that God was requiring of me were far beyond the limits of my comfort zone. He was stretching me because He knew that I was strong enough to endure the stretching. And by strong, I really mean weak. Within my own might, I am weak and can't perform some of the tasks that He desires. But through His strength and despite my weakness, He is accomplishing everything that He wants to through me.

But he said to me, "My grace is sufficient for you, for my power is made perfect in weakness." Therefore I will boast all the more gladly of my weaknesses, so that the power of Christ may rest upon me. 2 Corinthians 12:9 ESV

#GPMUOG – Anytime God is growing you, He is going to stretch you. It probably won't feel good because growing pains seldom do. Trust His process, follow His lead and forget what anyone thinks about your journey. You could really close the book right here because I just shared all the game with you! Hopefully, you are curious enough to want to know more about my crazy life to do so though!

Game From

The Pen

THIS BOOK IS DEDICATED TO WHOM?

If you actually took the time to read the first several pages of this book, then you saw that I dedicated this book to my Auntie Patricia. (You probably didn't read it though, so I will give you a few moments to go check it out. I'll wait…)

Saw it? Okay, good! To explain how this lady is my aunt and why I didn't know her as my aunt until I was a full adult would probably take this book and at least two more! But she is The Biological's aunt, which makes her my great-aunt. Now we don't have some super close relationship or anything, but for as long as I can remember, she has been telling me something to the effect of "I can't wait for The Book." You know how it goes. If I had one dollar for every time I heard her say that, I would be—naw, I still wouldn't be rich. But I would have about $43, give or take $10. If you think about it, that's still some pretty good change. Especially considering that we didn't meet until I was around 23 years old and haven't been in her presence for at least the last 7 years. (I meant what I said about it being a long story.) For the mathematically challenged and/or those who have no clue how old I really am, that's only about 7 years of face to face time. By my calculations, that adds up to at least 33 and as much as 53 prophetic confessions over my life. Some adults didn't receive that much positive affirmation during their entire adolescent years, but I did from Auntie Patricia. Auntie Patricia spoke, The Book, into existence at least 33, and as much as 53 times in only 7 years. God, you are amazing! If I could've captured every time I read or heard that from her, I would have just to substantiate this claim. Since I can't include them, you just keep on believing me. I haven't lied to you thus far.

One night in 2015, I was up vibing and writing and before I knew it, a dedication was flowing right from my ballpoint ink pen. Auntie Patricia's name was staring back at me, along with that of The Biological, who was already deceased at the time. Honestly, my first question was, "Why, God?" That not-so-rhetorical question was not really for Auntie Patricia as much as it was for The Biological. I mean why would God have me to dedicate my first New York Times Bestseller (name it and claim it!) to a man who tried to deny me? Because He knew where He had channeled the gift. As much as I love my Clutch Girl, I know this gift didn't come through her. It came from his lineage. My sisters on The Biological's side are phenomenal writers. Even his father can write. God wanted to exemplify what could be birthed from a place of rejection. No, I can't say from my personal experiences with him that The Biological was an amazing, stand-up man. He was full of you know what if you ask me. But the fact remains, without him there would be no me and the impact that I make through writing may have never been felt across nations. So for that, he made the dedication page.

Now Auntie Patricia saw The Book in me when I couldn't even see it and that's why she made the page! **#GPMUOG** – Always surround yourself with people who have vision beyond where you are currently standing. They can see where you are going much before you get there. Even if they are not lifetime journeymen, the confessions that they speak over your life will outrun you to your destiny.

Thank you, Auntie Patricia! You made the dedication page, but that wasn't enough. You deserved a whole chapter in The Book and this is still not enough... I hope this body of work makes you proud!

THE EVOLUTION OF A WRITER

There is just one last tidbit of information that I should share with you. This book highlights writings from as early as January 2016 and as late as well, whatever the FIRST published date reads. Emphasis on first because I am affirming that it will be in print multiple times in Jesus' Name! Because the authoring of this book spans such a long time, you will often see the maturity in my writing. When I went through my older writings, I worked very hard not to change anything. I wanted you truly feel what I felt when I was writing, but I also wanted you to be able to see the growth.

#GPMUOG – We sometimes expect so much so soon because everyone around us is only concerned with showcasing the end result but won't share the journey to get to that point. Seeing your growth process is what helps others grow. If they only see the fruit and not the planting, tilling, watering and cultivating, they immediately get discouraged. Getting only a glimpse of how quickly everything happened for you often leaves people feeling deflated because they know that would never happen like that for them. Meanwhile, it never happened like that for you either! Be honest with the people. The more we don't, the more selfish we become because our need to hide all our flaws, obstacles and idiosyncrasies is crippling those around us needing inspiration for their own journeys.

Game From

THE MAN

GOD IS POLITE; HE SPEAKS TO EVERYONE

Everyone can hear from God. He is polite and speaks to everyone. God even speaks to my 5-year-old, Kai. Kai talks to God; I am sure of it! One day she recounted a whole conversation that she had with Him by the ironing board. I was in awe, but I was not surprised at all, because like I said, God is polite!

Although He is polite and speaks to everyone, there is a still a process and various levels of understanding. Really deep church people will have you thinking that they have always been super deep, but it's a process. If you just accepted Jesus as your savior three days ago, you are not going to have the same type of relationship as someone who has been walking with Him for 25 years. It does not make their relationship better than yours in any way; there is just a deeper level of understanding. The higher you go, the more advanced you become at hearing His voice. Think about your romantic relationships. When you first meet a guy, you don't necessarily know his voice right away. Before there was caller ID, some of us were listening closely and choosing our words very carefully in the first few seconds of the conversation because we didn't know who we were talking to! We were still learning their voice.

When I first met my husband, I couldn't immediately recognize his voice. I was still learning it. But 16 years later I know his voice; I know his cough; I know his footsteps; I know his burp and every other absurd noise his body makes. That ability to recognize him without seeing him came with really getting to know him. I had to be exposed to more information. Hearing from God is very similar. The deeper your relationship gets with Him, the more you will recognize His voice. **#GPMUOG** – "I speak to you on your level. Stop coveting someone else's relationship with Me and work on building your own."

There are levels to this relationship thing. Naturally, most are looking to hear from God from the Mountain of Transfiguration levels (**Matthew 17:1-13**). But if you want to hear from Him on that level, you must go through some stuff. You only hear from Him on the mountain peak when you have spent majority of your time hearing from Him in the valley. **#GPMUOG** – It's the valley moments where God really speaks through your circumstances.

If you are in relationship with a man and you can't communicate with him because you don't hear or understand his voice, you would do whatever you could to rectify the situation. Your relationship with God is no different. He wants to hear from you and likewise, He wants you to be able to hear clearly from Him. I don't care if you are new to this thing and just started following Him yesterday when you picked up this book. He is amazingly smart, so He knows how to speak to you at your level. It may start off with simple situations where you're driving and praying for a parking space and BOOM! There's an empty space awaiting you right in front of your destination. That's not happenstance. That's God telling you that He hears you and He's got you!

Don't discredit those occasions. Coincidence is just God's way of remaining anonymous.

Sometimes He sends other people with messages. But be very cautious of what you accept from others. First off, what is their spirit like? You need to guard what you allow people to deposit into your spirit. Now your bank account is different; anyone can deposit there! I'm a firm believer that God doesn't have to always relay messages to me through other people though. We are way too close for that. My husband and I have the most intimate relationship here on earth. If he wants me to know something but he goes and tells his friend to tell me, we have just played the most ridiculous game of Telephone. My husband has access to me all day and he has my ear so why would he/should he have to always send messages through a friend? He should be able to bring it directly to me. The same is true with God. Anything He wants to say to me, He mostly says directly to me. If someone comes along with "a message from Lord," they are likely just confirming something that He has already told me.

Now, there will be times when He sends people with a word specifically crafted for you. Often He will have to send a confirmation because we need it to strengthen our faith or worse, we didn't listen the first time He told us. When we don't listen, He may have to send backup to reinforce what we heard the first time but didn't obey. For instance, when I tell one of my daughters to complete a chore such as taking out the trash and it goes undone, I may have to send one of her sisters to reinforce the message. She heard me the first time, but she didn't move so she has to hear the message again. Don't be like my daughters though. Heed His message the first time. **#GPMUOG** – When you don't move the first time (or maybe even the 2nd or 3rd time), God will send your brother or sister to confirm His word. Remember, delayed obedience is still disobedience.

Now, just like there are times when my husband *has* to go through other people to reach me (i.e. my phone may be dead, I may be in one of my deep sleeps, or maybe just maybe, there is limited cell service on my private veranda in the City of Love on a warm day in July as I sip the best fermented grapes from a local French winery…no, that's not it because he could just tell me because he would be right there beside me.) But just like those moments, there are some instances when God downloads your messages through other people. Many times, these are warnings of what's to come. Personally, I didn't start getting many of those types of messages until I didn't require as many confirmation messages before I obeyed. When He knew that He could trust me to obey in the present moment, then He could start entrusting me with limited information for the future. We can only be privy to limited information because our minds are way too small for anything more. Besides, only God truly knows what the future holds.

Sometimes He may speak to you through your dreams. In those instances, you will find that your dreams are extremely vivid and so real that you can almost touch the characters. Just know that it can only be a vision from God if it is something that God would actually tell you. If you are dreaming about the neighbor's husband and even if it feels so real, umm sorry ma'am, that's not God! This very thing happened to me in the past. Wait. Not the neighbor's husband thing! I am talking about dreams in general.

God came to me in my dream and revealed to me that the young fellow that I met on the block over a red cup of Grey Goose was indeed my husband. At the time we had just started seriously dating but in my dream, I was walking down the aisle in my wedding gown. I couldn't see his face as I pranced past all the guests. I could feel the anxiety though as my Daddy held my arm, but it wasn't the normal wedding day jitters. I was freaking out because I had no clue who was waiting for me at the end of that unusually long path. Once I finally got closer and took a squinted look, I realized it was him. It was my boyfriend. God spoke to me in that dream in an audible voice too. As clear as day, He said, "You are getting married on July 16, 2005."

I woke up covered in sweat with my heart racing two miles a minute. Whew! I thought. That was close. He almost got me! Marriage was not a part of my thoughts back then. I always imagined that I would get married in my mid-thirties. That dream came to me around September of 2004. By February of 2005, my boyfriend proposed and on July 16, 2005, I was married. God put me up on so much great game with this situation.

#GPMUOG – God is polite, and He speaks to everyone! So that includes you too, sweetie. If you feel as though you cannot hear from Him, I implore you to be like Jacob. (**Genesis 32:24-26**) Wrestle with

Him and don't let go until He blesses you with the ability to hear clearly. Remain in the mindset that He wants to do this for you. You cannot be in a relationship with anyone if you cannot effectively communicate with each other. The other lesson that I took away from this situation is that (wo)man makes plans and God changes those plans. You may have heard someone say, "If you want to make God laugh, tell Him your plans." I was so confident of how my life would turn out and it happened nothing like that. Yet, as much as I thought that I had carefully constructed the path for my life, the one He designed has been so much more rewarding than I could have ever imagined.

Naturally, when I started reluctantly telling people about my wedding dream, they thought I was crazy. Everyone, including my Clutch Girl, thought I was completely off my rocker. However, she's the one who gave me a handwritten note on my wedding day. It read, "We thought you were crazy, but I guess the joke's on us!" **#GPMUOG** – I don't care how ridiculously absurd it sounds to other people and even to you. If you know that you know that you know that God has told you something, then stand on that baby girl! He uses the foolish things of the world to confound the wise. (**1 Corinthians 1:27**)

He also speaks to me through my writings. I can whip out my laptop, my phone or my notebook and just start writing away as He pours out. He flows through my fingers as they glide the pen or press the keys because my gift is writing. If writing is not your gifting, then He may not speak to you in that

manner. However, He has gifted you with
something and He was intentional about the gifts
that He shared with you. He wanted you to use
them to get information from Him on how to love
His people, change the world and help the those in
need.

HE'S ALREADY ON THE SCENE

Other times, He just speaks in a soft subtle voice.
Then there are the days that a bulb just goes off and
you have that 'aha moment'. The last week in
January of 2017, I was standing in the middle of my
living room and found myself in a daze as I stared
into my reflection on the glass coffee table. Then it
hit me. Almost like a ton of bricks, but in a much
gentler way. At that very moment, I realized that I
wasn't going to be chosen for an opportunity that I
had applied for. I knew that gentle nudge was God
speaking to me. He was preparing me for the let-
down. It was as if He was saying, "Brace, yourself
baby girl because this is not going to end the way
that you desire." I remember softly praying, "Ok,
God. You already know that I am going to be
incredibly disappointed. But I know that You can
help me with that disappointment." Two days later
the email arrived, and I only briefly felt a tinge of
sadness. I was so grateful that He had warned me!
Since God had prepared me, I was ready.

Imagine there is a bad accident at a major
intersection nearest to your home. Two cars have
been involved in a head-on collision. The driver in
one of the vehicles has been ejected from the vehicle.

As he lies on the ground with blood flowing from his temples, every moment is crucial as he awaits medical assistance. What if the driver already knew that an accident was looming and called the paramedics before the impact? What if the ambulance was already there with the stretcher out, ready to receive the injured victim? If he is facing a life-threatening injury, those extras moments can change his life because the medics are already on the scene. He doesn't have to wait for help. I wasn't waiting for the help to arrive. He had already told me what was about to happen, and He was on the scene because I called Him. It doesn't mean that it hurt any less; it just means that He was present to soothe the pain. **#GPMUOG** – "You have to learn what disappointment feels like, so I will not allow you to get every opportunity that comes your way. If you listen closely, I will warn you so that you can prepare for the hit. If you put the ball back into My court, I can help you work through your pain and disappointment. I am here for you and it has always been My desire to help you."

WHEN HE TRUSTS YOU WITH THE GLORY...

Whenever I'm going through something heavy, I usually ask God why. (Because I do believe that I can ask Him questions. He's not obligated to answer, but I wouldn't dare be in an intimate relationship with anyone who I don't have the privilege to ask questions.) Like all those years that I had to watch my mother battle her drug demon. Or that time I was sexually assaulted by a close family member. And without a doubt, the scariest day of my life when I held my precious baby girl in my arms and she stopped breathing. Thankfully, my mother did a 180 and has been clean since 2009 and that one violation didn't turn into a repeat situation and I was able to resuscitate my Sweet Thang before any serious damage was done to her brain. During each of those trying events of my life, I found myself throwing my head back with tears streaming down my face, as I begged of God to tell me why I was I having to endure such pain. **#GPMUOG** – "Because I know that I can trust you with My glory. You ALWAYS tell people that I did it for you. And as long as you let me, I'm going to get the glory out of your life." So, if you feel like you're constantly going through something, it may be because He really trusts you with His glory. If you think you've been through more trials than the average person, consider yourself favored! God knows He can trust you with the story. You won't be afraid to open up and share it to aid in someone else's healing.

MY TWIN FRIENDS

Even when I was a hot mess, but I was serious about God, my twin friends were there. And when I say a hot mess, I was a hot, garbage mess! I was manipulative, sneaky, condescending and so much other yucky stuff. Side note: I am not condoning anything that I did in that period of my life, nor I am encouraging you to take that path. It was the journey I chose, and I am grateful to God that He kept me during that time. Now I understand why

He kept me. He had need of me. He had a great task that He needed me to carry out. **#GPMUOG** – "When I keep you, it is for your protection but also for My purposes. I have need of you. My twins, Grace and Mercy, are your friends."

Game From

The Man

GOOSE GETS YOU LOOSE

I met my husband on 103rd St., near Wentworth.
(If you are a girl from the far Southside of Chicago,
then you can probably envision this area well.) My
good girlfriend was stopping through to see her
then guy friend. Coincidentally, he was someone
that I had known for a while and I hooked her up
with him. I used to really think I was Cupid
Valentina because my last name was Love. Really!
Ask my friends how I acted up whenever I heard
my Love Day anthem. *Happy Valentine's Day!*
Every day is the 14th! (Outkast, Happy Valentine's
Day) I was (and still am) quite a piece of work!

So, this day her guy friend called and asked that
she stop by before we headed to the club. We got
over there and this cake (not the kind with icing and
candles) had a bouquet of flowers. (Please feel free
to insert that emoji with the huge googly, surprised
eyes.) Today roses are thoughtful and sweet. Back in
2002 on 103rd St., his boys were looking at him
sideways crazy and so was I. After all, we were in
the Wild Hunnids (Like Hundreds, but Hunnids).
Dudes were scattered on porches, milk crates, and
chairs that they brought out of their mama's houses.
Many were smoking weed and all were indulging in
alcoholic beverages. Where does romance and roses
comfortably fit into this equation?

But whatever; that was their twisted version of
some hood romance novel. Back to my story. We are
on 103rd and someone makes a liquor store run
around the corner to grab a bottle of Grey Goose.
(Southside girls, you may know precisely the liquor

store that I am referring to.) Now, if you knew Dime Bone (you'll learn more about her later if you don't know) from back in the day, then you are fully aware that Grey Goose was her libation of choice. Before every drinking session, she would proudly exclaim, "That Goose gets you loose!" Thank God for her deliverance!

Imagine this: I'm in the hood, on the block, drinking Grey Goose with my future husband. I may divulge more details of our initial meeting elsewhere, but just know it was not a love at first sight type of encounter. None of the events that day suggested that he would be the man that I spend a couple of forevers with. Of course, I didn't know he was my husband at the time. I didn't even know he would be a future dinner date. A more romantic environment is what I would have imagined for the first time meeting my husband-to-be. However, that chance occurrence is how God planned for our paths to cross. **#GPMUOG** – Your blessings may show up packaged much differently than you expect. Do not get so set on receiving your answered prayers the way that you think they should come. You will risk missing what God is trying to do in your life.

OUR PERFECT LOVE STORY

I was young, 24 to be exact, when I got married and I did not have it together at all. I'll be the first to admit that most of our issues early on in our marriage came from my immaturity. I had no clue about what being a wife meant. Truthfully, I had no idea who I was as a woman. I was still trying desperately to figure that out. The Man was so much more mentally and emotionally advanced than me. He knew exactly what he wanted when he saw me. *It don't take a whole day to recognize sunshine. (Common, The Light)* Since I was unsure of what I desired, I gave him a very hard time in the beginning. Roughly six months after we first met, he flew down to my school to visit me. During that trip, I treated him so badly. Honestly, if anyone ever treated me as harshly as I did him then (and for a long time afterward), I would've had a figurative funeral in their honor because they would surely be dead to me. But not The Man; he was unbelievably gracious and patient with me. When his weekend visit was just about over, he gave me a card that I have kept until this very day. In fact, I have all the cards that The Man has ever picked out for me. As a writer, I LOVE words, so cards truly make my heart pitter patter.

Anyway, he gave me a card on the day he was leaving. After an awful weekend of me ducking and dodging him, being a mean girl and just treating him so badly, he still thought enough of me to purchase me a card and a single rose. I am a sucka for a single rose. There is something so romantic about one rose standing alone. It's almost as if The Man was saying, "There are millions of women in the world but all I see is you. You are the single most beautiful rose." Well at least that's was what I conjured up in my head. The reality is probably more along the lines of $2 for a single rose vs. $30 for a dozen and the former beat out its opponent. The card that accompanied the rose is what left an indelible mark on my life though. I cannot recall verbatim what he wrote, but it said something like, "I don't know what happened this weekend, but I know God has me in your life for the long haul." Those words stop me in my tracks now. However, when I read them all those years ago, I thought he was nuts. But it was me. I was the crazy one.

Today, I am forever grateful that he saw something in me that was worth pursuing through my immaturity because I truly could not fathom what my life would be like if he was not in my corner. *Where would be if I didn't know? Who would I be if I didn't know you? (Kindred the Family Soul, Where Would I Be?)* It took me quite some time to really open up and grant him access to love me the way that I knew I deserved to be loved. Not only was I rejecting the beautiful love that he was extending toward me, I was also scared to show him how a real woman reciprocates love. I had previously poured from the depths of my heart and had given my love to so many others, that it left with me nothing but a depleted love tank. But that's what happens when you are sharing all your secrets with the wrong people. Men who do not see the value or who do not appreciate what you are sharing will easily toss you aside because they deem you as dispensable. **#GPMUOG** – Your love is valuable, and you must not allow anyone who cannot appreciate that value to force you to withhold that love from someone who will. That power is not theirs to have!

Needless to say, our early days were littered with challenges, bruised egos, and lots of figuring it out. Again, I raise my guilty hand because I was the one who was at fault for many of those issues. You know why? It was because I had been hurt so much and I never really took the chance to heal from that. My best girls joke all the time that I have never really spent time with myself. But they are telling the truth. I've always had a man. I love being in relationships, so I was going from one situation to the next. If I am brutally honest, a couple of those situationships overlapped. The line where one ended and the other began is blurred. Never taking a moment to simply pause and regroup only resulted in bags from one trip being carried over to the next destination. **#GPMUOG** – Spending time with yourself is instrumental in your growth. You cannot properly love another until you have found complete contentment with being and loving yourself.

As rocky as it was in the beginning, I would not exchange it for a do-over. Those days built the character of our marriage. They taught us invaluable lessons about loving each other at our most unlovable stages. They proved to me just how committed The Man was to his call to love me perfectly. He could have easily thrown his hands up in disgust and ran in the other direction, but he held on to me instead. The Man held tightly to what God had shown him even when my actions expressed that I wanted to be everything but held on to. That's how I knew that he was a true man of God, after His own heart. God did that very thing for me. He held onto to me because he knew how messed up I was. God knew that I needed Him for where I was going, and He loved me too much to let me go. The Man followed that example. Thank God he did because he helped to write our perfect love story. *Who wants that perfect love story anyway? Cliché, cliché, cliché... (Beyoncè/Jay-Z, Part II)*

#GPMUOG – Your love story may not look like a conventional fairy tale but as long as it has been orchestrated by a perfect God, your love story is perfect for the two of you.

MARRIED FOLKS MIND THEIR OWN MARRIAGES

"Do you think married people should have joint bank accounts?" "Who should be responsible for the bills? The husband or the husband and wife?" "Who should discipline the children?" "Who should do this; who should do that?" Shut up with all these questions! I absolutely hate when people ask how married people should live their lives. **#GPMUOG** – Married people should do what works for that married couple. Outside of the basic rules of loving, respecting, honoring, providing, sexing, and remaining faithful to your spouse, there are no other cookie cutter models. Do love your way and if it's working for you and God is pleased, you don't need answers from anyone. That's it, that's all!

MY HUSBAND GOT GAME TOO

(Ladies, this is where it is okay to pass the book to your man.)

Men, this book was not written for you, but I know your women are going to make you read it at some point or try to read excerpts to you. I also know that you are going to pretend like you don't want to but read it anyway! They will especially want you to read this part because it will be of benefit to them! Since you will be forced to read, here are a few suggestions that I want to share with you to make your life a little easier.

Take cues from your woman. Listen to what she says and what she doesn't say. That's inside and outside of the bedroom. Sometimes we do not want to bruise your ego, so we won't tell you if something is wrong. This rule applies to both emotional and sexual issues. If you watch our body language you will know when something needs to be changed. I know I just angered some man is who is reading this. You are thinking, "No, a real, strong woman would just say what she needs." Let me say it again for the men in the back. Sometimes we do not want to bruise your ego so we won't tell you if something is wrong. Did you hear it that time?

When we do share our issues with you, respond as if they matter to you! We are expressing concern because we need your assistance working through them. After all, you are a crucial part of this equation and without your effort, things just don't add up. Early on in our marriage, I dealt with a lot of insecurities as it pertained to The Man. I struggled with thoughts that he didn't trust me to make sound decisions concerning our family. After verbalizing my concerns one day, he was a bit angered and surprised because he couldn't understand where those feelings were emerging from. Despite that confusion, he worked arduously at ensuring that I had no reason to feel that way. **#GPMUOG** – Men, it is your responsibility to help us navigate through our insecurities toward you. Even if you feel like they are for no valid reason, you still must assist in the healing process. Unless you don't care about the relationship, then listen to the rest of the world; they will send you off by telling you that it's solely her problem to deal with.

There will be also times when you may feel as if she is not considering your feelings. We tend to think that because you are men that you don't have emotions. Thus, we put everything in front of you or use sex as a pawn or completely neglect you when we are working (or specifically in my case, writing a book.) *I neglect you when I'm working. When I need attention, I tend to nag. I'm a host of imperfections and you see past all that. (Beyoncé, Flaws and All)* When The Man knows that I am going through or I am pushing myself too hard to the point that our relationship is suffering, then he does something to get me back on track. He runs me a warm bath to soothe my nerves. Instead of allowing me to stay up all night writing and working, he lights candles and engages me in pillow talk. Helping me, ultimately helps him, if you know what I mean. Alrighty, that's all the good game for you. You can return the book to her now. I'll wait...

I'm still waiting! Why are you still reading? Because you are just as nosey as you try to make us out to be! Fine! Stay, but don't get mad at what I am about to say.

I got him right together for you, girl! Now if you don't see any improvements, he is just being rebellious! I'll deal with that in the next book. Now it's your turn. Stop listening to everything that everyone tells you. You know that quote, "A man is not worth your tears and the one who is will never make you cry?" Yea, that's a bunch of BS! Whoever said that was clearly never married. I don't think they've been anyone's girlfriend either. Because, baby, your husband is going to make you cry and not just once during the journey of your marriage. He is not perfect, and he is going to make some mistakes that will hurt you. Some will be surface; others may cut a bit deeper. The truth is that he occupies space in your heart and anyone who can get that close to you at some point will probably cause you to cry. It's not the end of the world though. **#GPMUOG** – Stop comparing your relationship to the stuff that you see on television or the #relationshipgoals memes on social media. All real marriages are going to experience some cold winter seasons and some bleak valley moments.

FREQUENT, BOMB SEX

Scoot in a little closer because I have to share a dirty little secret with you. (Men, I thought I told you to STOP reading! Umm hmm, I see you!) This little church girl is a freak and I am not ashamed to say so. If given the opportunity, I would stand atop Mount Everest with a bullhorn and scream to the nations, "All women, activate your inner whore!" Wait, don't start judging me now! I told you from the beginning that I was going to share my truth with you so don't go clutching your pearls now. Kristen is just on a mission to save these sexless marriages, one arched back at a time. After all, most of you married women (including myself) used to be hanging from chandeliers getting it in when you were single. Now someone has pledged their eternal love to you and backed it up with factual actions by marrying you and you're under the cover every night with your onesie pajamas on acting like the prude you know you're not! Stop letting the devil trick you! You may have a strange case of déjà vu later as will definitely be visiting this topic a few times. It's important! And trust me, your husband won't mind if I drive this point home a few more times.

Married men and women have a license to do whatever they please in their bedroom or car or laundry room or private deck or wherever the heck they please. The only things that are off limits are sinful acts. So that means no other people, same sex or opposite, should be in the marital bedroom because then you are committing adultery. And yes, it is still adultery even if your partner is fully aware and engaging in the act. That crosses another boundary and opens you to demons that you may not even be prepared to slay. Everything else is up to the husband and wife. So be as open and free as you both desire and run from any person, lay or clergy, who tries to put parameters on the sexual activities of you and your spouse.

The Man once told me that I could do anything that I wanted to do with and to him sexually. When he said that I knew he had completely yielded himself to me in that regard. I don't care what people want you to think. It's not just the man's heart and mind that you need to capture. Baby, you need to captivate his sexual appetite too! **#GPMUOG** – Frequent, bomb sex can help your man through some of the roughest patches of life. Even if he has the boss from hell, if he knows that he is coming home to great sex, that man will do whatever it takes to make it through that day. And yes, for all you deep ones, I know he will keep pushing at work because he has a family to support. But plugging into his source is going to keep him going.

Your husband has multiple ways to plug into God and you happen to be one. Women are direct connections to God and we are the closest to man than any other being roaming this earth. Eve was formed from a rib dissected from Adam's anatomy. How much closer do you get than that? Don't deny your husband the opportunity to get plugged in, especially when he needs it the most. When we were in one of the worst financial struggles of our marriage, we found ourselves making love almost daily. That was an outlet for my husband who, outside of those moments when we were engaging, would spend hours with his mind consumed with how we were going to make ends meet. **#GPMUOG** –Some of your greatest growth spurts in marriage will come from frequent, bomb sex too!

The wife does not have authority over her own body, but the husband does. And likewise, the husband does not have authority over his own body, but the wife does. Do not deprive one another except with consent for a time, that you may give yourselves to fasting and prayer; and come together again so that satan does not tempt you because of your lack of self-control. 1 Corinthians 7:4-5 NKJV

#SupportIsSexy

On my 36th birthday, I received hundreds of social media messages wishing me happy birthday. I would be telling you the first lie of this book if I said that I remember all those messages. Even the most touching ones became fleeting thoughts shortly after I read them. However, there was this one that made a lasting impression on me. This couple clearly gets up every day and scours Facebook for anyone celebrating a birthday. The couple left a personalized message on my wall along with a link to their music. It read something like, Happy Birthday Kristen from complete strangers with a link to some amazing music. Talk about speaking the language of a music head! Of course, I clicked, and I was jamming to their music. All the while, I was thinking that those two were absolute geniuses! I believe I got more excited about the couple using my birthday as an innovative marketing campaign than the smooth grooves or the personalized message. I was so excited that I told my husband, but of course he didn't get half as excited as I did because he isn't wired like me. He looked at me and said, "Oh okay. That's nice." I could've gotten mad like I have many times in the past. However, I have learned many valuable lessons on this entrepreneurship road. If people are not passionate about your dream they are simply not going to be passionate about your dream. That doesn't mean that they don't support YOU because they are not passionate about specifically what you are doing. They just don't love it the way that you love it. But they love you and the way that you love your dream, so they support you 100%. God was truly the one who had to put me up on that game. That really freed me to allow my husband to be who he was, not who I thought he should be.

When I wanted to write, he let me write. We would sit together, and he watched TV, but he let me write. He let me be who I was, not who he wanted me to be. That's how you support someone that you love. As leery as he was, he went along with my plan. Why? Because He trusted God and He trusted the God in me. Your spouse, your family or even your friends are not always going to rock with your ideas. Sometimes they are not going to understand why you are doing what you are doing. I know my husband was utterly confused when I told him that I wanted to stop accepting orders for my very successful dessert company and channel my energy into writing, speaking, and empowering women. My husband is a bottom line kind of guy so all he really wanted to know was, "what about the money?!" I told him, "I know you don't understand, but just trust God because I know He's leading me." If you are looking for some support along the way as you pursue your dreams, get God on your team. You can only get the type of trust that you are looking for from your family and friends when they know that your relationship with God is real. My husband knew that as far-fetched as my ideas sounded, God was behind them. He trusted the God in me. **#GPMUOG** – Get God on your team; He can fight for you and convince your circle that your ideas are gold. He will help them see your vision. He will also reveal who is not even worth the convincing.

Married people, when you are trying to give birth to something, it is imperative that the two of you are on one accord. The word asks, **"How can two walk together unless they agree?" (Amos 3:3)** When God was showing me a glimpse vision for my family, my career and my ministry, He told me to go to my husband and asked if He truly felt like I was hearing from God. That was a scary conversation to have because I was nervous to hear his response. However, the conversation needed to be had. If he wasn't on the same page as me, we would have to figure out how to rectify that. As much as you think that you can grow beyond what your spouse thinks, if you two are operating with different objectives in mind, then the team is always going to suffer.

One day I made the mistake of asking God why I was dealing with this issue of support with my husband. **#GPMUOG** – "Girl, I am putting you through this entire ordeal with your husband because it is going to make great content for your book. You already know that I put you through stuff just to give you a story to share to help somebody else." Welp, here it is. I pray that it helps you through your circumstances!

CHOOSE BATTLES

If you have ever been in a relationship, then you already know that no one can push your buttons like your significant other. There is usually not another single person who can cut you the way that they can. That person is the closest to you and has access to you that others don't. For that reason, they can hurt you in ways that you never imagined being hurt. *Saying I love you is giving you strength to break my heart, but I'm trusting you not to. (Mary J. Blige, Don't Mind)* After one of the biggest arguments that our marriage had ever endured, both my husband and I found ourselves with bruised egos and anguished feelings. Due to both my overly competitive nature and my intense anger in the moment, I verbalized some things that could have potentially damaged us forever. In the heat of the moment, my husband stepped outside of himself and came right back for me. His words and tone pierced the depths of my soul. Truthfully, I don't even recall what the blowup was about, and I am sure that it started off as something so minuscule and irrelevant. You know those arguments, right? The ones where your retrospective reflections reveal a dumb question or statement as the starting point. "Why would you put the spoon in the fork compartment?" "I find it really funny that you keep eating all the Colby Jack cheese and only leaving the Provolone and you know I hate Provolone." (Please note: when statements start with "I find it really funny," the person delivering the message doesn't find any comic relief in the situation at all. I'm giving you that one for free!)

So, after this huge argument that probably originated from me fussing about him using my Pond's Cold Cream (because this really has been a point of contention in the past — don't you dare start judging me now), I came back and apologized for all the emasculating and dehumanizing things that I said. He said he forgave me, but I was waiting for his apology too. It didn't come in the time frame that I determined that it should. My insides were burning to bring it up to him but instead, I prayed about it. **#GPMUOG** – Choosing your battles means seeking God about which things are necessary to pursue. When it's indeed your battle, God will create an environment conducive for you to address the issues. He didn't give me that opportunity in that instance but moving past that painful point was much more important than me trying to coerce an apology.

You may be giving me a major side-eye right now, thinking that you would've had to say something because your voice was going to be heard. Yep, I said all of that too. Yet at the end of the day, it was His guidance that I chose to follow. Choose your battles wisely and always refer back to the number one piece of game. Always follow God's way, even when it's unpopular among people. Even if one of them is you.

MAKESHIFT WALLS & ALL

In our home, which we have long ago outgrown, our bedroom is literally adjacent to my girls' bedroom. Being right next door to my children has made having sex a challenge. However, we haven't let that stop us. We just got creative. Honey, don't you let the devil use you to deny your husband of sex. Whatever circumstances you are facing, you better get creative with it! If you don't know what to do, Google your exact situation and get an answer! "How to have good sex in a studio apartment when me, my husband and the kids are all sleeping in the living room?" Girl, Google knows everything! They will have you constructing a makeshift wall and door in the corner somewhere! Don't play with me! #GPMUOG – There will always be less than ideal circumstances. It is your job to figure how to make the best of those circumstances. Use whatever you have been given and work the heck out of it! Watch how God hooks you up with more when you learn how to use and appreciate the less.

Soon enough, I'll be telling you who are reading this, thank you. Thank you because after ___ years in this house, we can move! I no longer have to sneak to engage with my husband because we have a private master suite with soundproof walls! I don't know when, but I know He is going to show up!

Game From

The Parentals

NEED IS NEED

The Bible tells us to despise not humble beginnings and humble beginnings are truly where I come from. You may not fully comprehend just how humble I mean, so let me Picasso the picture for you. Yes, Picasso is synonymous with the verb 'paint.' **#GPMUOG** – When you are the best at something, your name becomes one with what you create. Google is a thing but everyone 'Googles' what they need to know because Google is the best! You can also become an adjective for the same result – The Kristen Effect.

Ok, back on the ranch! A note from my mother in my baby book reads, "Happy first birthday. Mommie was poor this birthday so you didn't even have a birthday cake. But I promise to make it up to you next year." It's so interesting to me that I didn't have a birthday cake on my first birthday because at 37 years old, I am so adamant about having a birthday cake for everyone's celebration. To me, it's not a birthday if there is no cake!

However, the bigger question that I have is if my mama didn't have money for a cake, how come no one gave her $10 to buy one? Had they already helped her out so much that purchasing a cake was out of the question? Did someone offer to buy a cake, but she politely declined because she didn't want people to pity her? Those are very plausible theories, but I really don't think either offers the real explanation. Without any confirmation from my mama, I am almost certain that she didn't have it and she didn't ask anyone either. Her pride kept her silent and in turn, probably made her feel like the most inadequate parent ever. But she could've just asked. Asked her mother, my beloved grandmother. Asked her sister, my favorite aunt. Asked her best friend, my giving Godmother. How come she just didn't ask? Because she is I and I am she! The apple didn't fall too far from the tree on this one. She was so caught her up in her pride that it was keeping her from getting what she needed/wanted. It seems as if I inherited and enhanced that flaw. I wear it on my sleeve for everyone to know that I may need help, but I would not dare open my mouth and ask anyone to do anything for me.

We can get so caught up in our pride that we will not ask for what we need. One of the most profound lines that I've heard in a movie was spoken in *Concussion*. In response to a young lady who declined a financial offer, Will Smith's character answered, "Need is not weak. Need is need." We all have a point in our lives when we are in need. It may be a financial need, a spiritual need such as prayer, a physical need like a helping hand or maybe you just need someone to talk to. Regardless of the nature of the need, we all will find ourselves in the "I got a need" line.

When I was flat out broke and completely struggling, I had no help but that's only because no one knew I had a need. I was prideful, shameful and a host of other -fuls. I was so worried that people would think that I was a failure that I never opened my mouth and asked for anything. Well you know what God says: "You have not because you ask not." And you know what *they* say, "A closed mouth don't get fed." Who are *they* anyway?

The ones who cared the most about me and the least about my failures couldn't even help me because they were not aware of the need.

#GPMUOG – Being too prideful to ask for help hinders the giver's blessing too. When you do not make room in your life to receive the blessings from God through other people, you don't allow them to release what they have so God can send more into their hands. Keeping quiet about your need doesn't just affect you. Oddly enough, it is the Kristens of the world who are the most giving yet find it the most difficult to be on the receiving end.

#GPMUOG – As a natural giver, if you don't ever open your arms to receive then you are operating in a spirit of control. You always want to be needed by others but never helped in return. Quickly reject that spirit and get back in your rightful place.

The bottom line is that you should never confuse having a need with being needy. It's nothing to be ashamed about. We all have a need at some time or other. That's why God created Adam and Eve. He knew that you would have a need that He could only meet through someone other than yourself. That's why Eve is Adam's helpmeet. She is helping God meet a need in Adam's life. And before you Bible thumpers, go getting all deep on me, I know that God doesn't need any help! But I also know that He carries out His purposes for His people through His people!

DADDY IS NOT DADDY?

I am convinced that many individuals do not understand that the decisions that they make today are going to impact the people around them a hell of lot a more than they will ever affect the actual individual. The family tree inside the front cover of my baby book provides a crystal-clear indication of the type of dysfunction that I was born into. You can plainly see that my mama used some old school Paper Mate Wite Out-yes Wite Out- to change the name listed on the father line. The names on the paternal grandparents line are also whited out. Although my mother did not present my book to me until I brought home my first child, I was exposed to the truth behind the old school white out over 25 years ago.

At the most awkward of age of 10, I got a piece of news that could've changed the trajectory of my entire life for the worse, but it didn't. It should've changed my life, but I just think God has His Special Assignment Angels (SAAs) on my case. I am sure I wore those SAAs out, especially in my high school and college years!! In fact, I am probably still wearing my SAAs out!

I vividly remember playing outside on a beautiful summer day. The pink handlebar streamers were flapping in the wind as I raced down the block. I used to love bikes with streamers that hung from the handlebar and that flowed in the wind as I was riding. I imagined the wind was hitting my face and that I would experience that exact feeling one day in my convertible as I cruised down the shoreline of the Pacific while the wind slapped my face. I have always been a dreamer! The only problem with that dream now is that I barely ride with the windows down in my car. I don't want my hair getting messed up. Don't judge me! You know how we are about our hair, Sisters!

I really hope you are keeping up with this story! So, I ended up running into The Biological on my grandmother's block. By "running into," I may have literally run him over because I hadn't been riding a bike for too long before that. His mother lived right across the street from my maternal grandmother. I am positive this made the environment conducive and convenient for the easy hookup and the conception of this here legend! Anyway, he approached me while I was outside playing and introduced himself. He then went on to say, "Krissy, would you believe me if I told that we were related?" Too occupied with getting back to playing, I said, "Yea, yea, yea I know!" I had no idea what he was talking about and quite frankly I didn't care. I am certain that given their history, he knew my mama to be crazy as all outdoors and decided that he was better off alive by not going any further with the conversation. He ended with, "Tell your mama Keith said hi." And just like that, I was off in the wind again, cruising down the Pacific shoreline. That night when I returned home, I told her exactly what he said. My mother is a medium brown complexion, but in that moment her face was almost a pale white. I stood studying her, trying to figure out what was wrong. She didn't explain until the next morning as I was getting ready for school. It was a very casual conversation and she simply said, "That guy you met yesterday is your real father." I said ok and went on about my morning ritual. She must've thought that it was going to have a detrimental impact on me because she drafted a letter to my teacher explaining everything and requesting that the school counselor see me. I opened the letter before I got to school and ripped it up. I was good. I didn't need counseling. As far as I was concerned my Daddy was still my daddy! I have always been resilient (and nosey)!

#GPMUOG – Understand that sometimes people who really love you (especially your parents) will feel as though the best thing for you is to not share certain information with you. It is your mother's job to protect you. My mama felt that she was protecting her baby by withholding information from me about The Biological. Please don't hold it against them for having your best interest at heart, even if you would have done things drastically differently.

The mess that The Biological created was more than a notion. When I was about 16, he picked me up and took me out to lunch. It was quite awkward because I really knew much of nothing about the man. On our way home, he shared with me exactly how he came to be the daddy that got whited out in the baby book.

"Your mother took me to court for child support. The judge looked me square in my eyes and asked if you were my daughter. I stared him right back with a straight face and said that it is highly unlikely." At that exact moment, I knew that any chance of a relationship that he was trying to kindle was never going to happen. I was feeling like Jesus: if you deny me, I will deny you before the father! The interesting thing is that I wasn't hurt by it at all. I had no resentment. I was just happy to finally know the truth. For me, life was good because I had my Daddy and a family attached to my Daddy. A huge family, might I add. (He had a total of 10 brothers and sisters.) God isn't lying when He tells you that He will restore what the enemy tried to steal. It comes back greater, later! So really, that denial did nothing TO me, but it did something FOR me; made me stronger!

#GPMUOG –There will be times when God knows that what you need is not what you currently have. So, he will send a replacement. The replacement is much better than what you could have ever imagined the original to be. So much so that you don't even realize that there was a void caused by the original. This precisely describes my circumstances with my Daddy. No, he is not my biological, but he is my real daddy! I thank God often that He chose someone to do the job that another couldn't or wouldn't.

GENERATIONAL BLESSINGS

Our author/reader relationship kicked off with me explaining why I would have music Tourette's here and there. Honestly, I cannot help it. It is embedded in my DNA; I am a certified music head! I believe my love of music originated from my Clutch Girl and was cultivated by my Daddy. For years, one of the many songs that pushes me over into sheer happiness is by my boy Stevie.

Until the rainbow burns the stars out in the sky. Always. Until the ocean covers every mountain high. Until the dolphin flies and parrots live at sea. Always. Until we dream of life and life becomes a dream. (Stevie Wonder, As)

Whenever I hear those lyrics and that infectious, accompanying melody, I instantly feel a strong connection to anyone I deeply love. Well duh! It's probably because, Stevie belts out, "I'll be loving you always." That theory made sense until I was I chauffeuring my Clutch Girl around one winter day. As the song came on, *"Doo Doo Doo Doo..."* I went right into my side to side snapping and grooving. While I was enjoying my jam, I noticed my Clutch Girl gazing out the window with a slight grin that suggested that the song meant something to her as well. It was almost as if she knew I was about to ask her if she loved this song as much as I did, because she turned to me and explained the value that the song held. "This was playing in my hospital room as I was laboring and trying to push you out." Wow, my Clutch Girl literally birthed me into my love for music!

However, it was my Daddy, who fostered that love and helped it to grow. When I was a little girl, he would always have some music playing no matter what he was doing. Washing his car, cooking, taking a shower, whatever. Last summer, I visited him in Georgia and he had his stereo going the entire time that I was there. When I went to bed, the old school melodies of the O'Jays or Whispers would lull me to sleep. When I woke up at 6:00 am, he was already up cooking breakfast and you guessed it, listening to music. Really dude?!

No, wait; I have an even better one. Back in the day, my Daddy would be actively watching the television but have the volume turned all the way down, so he could listen to music! I never quite wrapped my mind around that one. Now as an adult, I recognize that as the side chick syndrome. He may be interested in what's going on with the both of you, but trust, somebody is being turned all the way down because he's listening to the side chick. However, even when he's not listening to the main woman, he's watching her, making sure she's ok because he would never want her to know that he hurt her. He doesn't care if the sidechick knows because, well — she's a sidechick. Now that is some good game straight from God. I am not even smart enough to think of that analogy on my own.

My Daddy's obsession with music is thoroughly understood by me. I don't need any sort of an explanation. Music sparks all type of nostalgia. You can hear a song and instantly remember what you were doing, who you were with, where you were headed and how you felt inside. There is not a single other thing that does that for me. Music is magical to me. I turn music on to do everything, even sometimes sleep. So, I get it and really, I am he and he is me. Even though I don't have my Daddy's blood running through my veins, I spent enough time with him that his hobbies became mine. I have his DNA without even having his genes. That's deep, right? **#GPMUOG** – Be careful who you spend your time with because inevitably, you begin to inherit characteristics of the ones you hang around consistently.

I once dated a music head just like me. I thought that our love for music was divinely inspired. I had someone who had an intense affair with melodies and we could enjoy it together. When I married somebody who loved movies more than he loved music, I was utterly confused and a bit disappointed. "What about somebody who loves what I love, God?" I whined like a baby, but every time I ask, He always answers. **#GPMUOG** – "No, child. You don't have to marry someone just like you. The beauty of love and marriage is exposure and teaching him to see the world through your eyes and vice versa."

WHEN MY CLUTCH GIRL MET STANLEY

I made my very first car purchase near the end of 2000. I was sticking my chest out so proudly because I used my own cold, hard cash to buy that car. It was a 1991 Nissan Stanza. He was shiny, black and on point. I immediately named him Stanley! There was so much pride wrapped up in that car that I drove it from school in Alabama back home to Chicago. The moment I pulled up and my Clutch Girl saw my vehicle, her eyes lit up. She grabbed one of her friends out of the house and showed her my new whip. Her urgency to do so spoke volumes of her pride in my accomplishment. It didn't matter that my car was 10 years old. It didn't matter that there were over 100,000 miles on my car. It didn't even matter that I wouldn't have that car for a full three months before the transmission went out. *I bought an '85 Cutlass on some dane-a-danes. Now I'm the ish, huh? The motor blew in 30 days. (T.I., Still Ain't Forgave Myself)*

None of those pieces of information was relevant in that moment. All that mattered was that I was proud of what I had accomplished, and my Clutch Girl was too. **#GPMUOG** – You need people around you who celebrate your achievements, no matter how small. Pray for cheerleaders and supporters who are eager to brag about you to their circles. Those are the cheers that keep you pressing when you want to throw in the towel. Contrary to what most want you to believe, we all need some cheers along this race. Don't apologize for that.

Game From

The Crew

DON'T LET THE DEVIL PUNK YOU

Do you ever allow someone to shut you down
and stop you from sharing what you know as truth?
I thought I was above this behavior, but I realized
very quickly that I can allow what others say to shut
my mouth. I have a friend who I will call Meeka.
Meeka is such a kind-hearted individual who does
so many great things to impact the lives of others.
Meeka knows and loves God but something that she
said one day really rubbed me the wrong way.
Meeka publicly announced on Facebook that she
didn't believe that the devil was real. Argh! Let me
clear this up for you right now! The devil is real. He
is not some fiery red fictional character with horns
coming out of his head, a long tail and a pitchfork
nestled in his right hand. No, that is not him at all.
But there is a devil out here going to and fro looking
for who he can devour. He is relentless in his
pursuit of canceling your destiny and he is very
committed to his three jobs. I know this concept
may be hard to grasp for many of you because you
aren't even committed to one job but he is managing
three and unfortunately, doing a great job. He is
killing, stealing and destroying lives.

Now you would probably think that since I just
effortlessly laid that simplistic explanation out for
you, that I surely shared the same or more with
Meeka. Well, you are wrong! I was so concerned
with saving my friendship and favorable stance
with Meeka that I said nothing. What a disservice I
did to Meeka. She may or may not have accepted
my correction, but I would have only found that out

with a conversation.

The even greater disservice was to countless others and to myself. I allowed that comment to shut my mouth. To not offend Meeka and her beliefs, I chose my words carefully. I stopped posting many of my **#GPMUOG** posts on Facebook because I was trying to keep Meeka comfortable. Of course, this is when God was sending all type of revelation about the enemy and his plans. Yet, I didn't share them because of what my friend said. You already know God checked my butt good and then He gave me this good game! **#GPMUOG** – "You cannot go along just to get along. Recognize that the enemy will attempt to shut you down and will often use those who are connected to you to do so. Don't you ever allow your desire to keep someone (including yourself) comfortable to outweigh your desire to do what I instructed you to do."

#BetterGetYouAChancee

Friends. How many of us have them? (Whodini, Friends) I really wish that I had some fancy words to describe how I feel about my Bestie, but me trying to come up with words that do her justice would only fail. This girl is the epitome of all friends. If there were a training class on how to be a phenomenal friend, I am certain that she would be on the curriculum development board. She is such a great friend that I often compliment her on her friend capabilities by reminding her that she is a much better friend that I could ever be. I don't go as far as to say that I don't deserve her because I deserve all the finer things in life, including top shelf friends. But, I do aspire to be as an amazing friend as she is one day.

I have no problem admitting that I am not always the greatest listener. It is not because I don't want to listen, but I think that sometimes my brain is so overloaded with all the things that I have to do or have going on that I cannot accept any new information. It is like my ears just reject all incoming requests. Not my Bestie though. She is a great listener and offers sound advice. Now her remembering what she told you is another story. Her memory is sucky! Hey, I guess you can't win them all! **#GPMUOG** – Friends are great listeners.

One July, I was in a bit of a financial bind. My Bestie deposited $150 into my account. Initially, I thought it was a just-because love offering since she was privy to what was going on in my life. I later realized that my friend sent me money right before my anniversary. She wanted me to be able to enjoy myself. She desired for me to be able to put a smile on my husband's face with a thoughtful gift. I told you, my Bestie is the bomb! **#GPMUOG** – Real friends want your marriage to work. The only caveat is if your spouse is mistreating you. Then, your friends only want you to work on getting out of that thing because they love you and will murder that fool for treating you below excellence.

That same Bestie edited my entire first book. She didn't ask me for anything. Not one dime. But she knew I couldn't afford it anyway. However, she knew if she helped me finish my book, I would be that much closer to my destiny. **#GPMUOG** – Real friends assist you with DPAs. (Destiny Promoting Activities) They get genuinely excited when they witness you walk into your God-given destiny.

I love that my Bestie is a woman who knows the power of prayer and is not afraid to exercise that power for my benefit. One of the greatest examples of this power at work in our friendship was when my Sweet Thang was sick. My Bestie was at home praying for my baby. She was on the phone praying with me. My Bestie is so dope that she even arranged an entire prayer chain for us during that time. To this day, I cannot trace every single person who was fervently praying for my child and my Bestie is a large piece of that. Prayer is such an integral piece of our relationship. Throughout our 15 years of friendship, there have been weekly prayer calls scattered about. On those early morning calls, we would alternate praying for each other. Unfortunately, our consistency is not up to par with our friendship skills, so we always fall off. Yet, we always eventually pick right back up where we left off. **#GPMUOG** – Real friends pray for and with you. Period.

The bottom line is that friends should be adding rich equity to your life and vice versa. Yes, my Bestie is still a much better friend than I could ever be to her. However, I work very hard at being what she needs me to be in this relationship. Wait; let me say this in caps so that you don't miss it. FRIENDSHIP IS WORK! Yes, that's some of that good game that God gave me. No hashtag necessary because I screamed it at you and I am positive that you copied! #BetterGetYouAChanceè!

SEASONAL FRIENDS

That reminds me that I was close to a friend for a season. Wow, until just now I didn't realize that I even had seasonal friends. I mean I hear the phrase all the time, but I really thought that didn't apply to me. All my friends have become forever friends. Maybe their position moved from inner circle to the third ring, but they were still forever friends. But this one was different. **#GPMOUG** – People are in your life for a reason, season or a lifetime. It is your charge to learn how to discern the difference and be okay when the relationship has run its course.

When Diamond and I grew really close she was going through a tumultuous time in her marriage. She found herself disrespected, rejected, and the victim of a blatant adulterer. I did what I could to support her in her marriage and with her kids. By some sure act of God — because only God could have turned that frog into a prince — her husband had a sudden and unbelievable turnaround. As far as I know (which is not far, might I add), it's for real too. Of course, they got back together and started finally living their happily ever after. Diamond had her man back, but at the same time, I lost a friend. Just as sudden as his transformation, she disappeared from my life. The calls and visits stopped abruptly. It was clear since she no longer needed me to whine to and watch her children and pray with her that she dropped me like her husband had previously dropped her.

I must admit that I got all wrapped up in my feelings about it for a moment. I even texted Diamond one night and apologized for not being a better friend. She hit me with some random emoji like the kissy face or some fake smile. Mmmm kay, that didn't go as I expected. However, the more I thought about it, I wasn't the bad friend; she was. Girl, it's like after your relationship got tight, you no longer needed the one who was praying, talking you through, and being whatever support you needed. Bump your kissy face; insert the rolling eyes here!

Or maybe it wasn't my fault or hers. Maybe that's just how God designed our season. I had done my job and bestowed my big sister wisdom. Now it was time to move on. The relationship had run its course and we both had to be ok with that. **#GPMUOG** - We must know when it's time to move on from relationships, whether it's romantic relationships, friendships, and even familial-ships. Remember, if God told you to move, you need to trust that it's putting you in a better position.

"When people can walk away from you, let them walk... Your destiny is never tied to anyone who left... People leave you because they are not joined to you..." (Bishop T.D. Jakes, Nothing Just Happens)

RED HEARTS OVER RED BOTTOMS

One of The Man's female friends put a bad taste in my mouth for a minute. He came home one evening feeling deflated because she told him how he needed to get me a pair of red bottoms. He didn't say anything about feeling some type of way about it, but he kept talking about the conversation, so I knew it bothered him.

Sure, he could've blown his whole paycheck on some red bottoms but for what? I looked my husband straight in the face and said, "I've never put those type of demands on you." I didn't put that kind of pressure on him because I knew we couldn't afford that. If you are truly supporting your husband as his rib-mate as he's leading your home and family, you aren't putting any unnecessary pressure on him for ish that doesn't matter. Birkin bags, Giuseppes and Porshe rides don't matter. They don't last. But if you all choose to go broke to build a business or write a book or help a cause, then you have planted on fertile ground. **#GPMUOG** – Stop putting unreasonable demands on your man. If you know you can't afford Louboutins then stop asking for Louboutins. Yes, you very well may deserve a pair, but you deserve those shoes when you can afford to pay for them. That's not a necessity purchase. Let that man take care of business because you also deserve to have a roof over your head. But if you keep on requesting stuff you know you can't afford, you won't even have that. To the woman who doesn't want anything but love, a man will give her the entire world. *I gotta chick that loves me and she'll do anything for me that's why I fux with her. (Tyrese, I Gotta Chick)* Sure, I probably could have chosen a more romantic love song for this portion of the soundtrack, but I know that by now you have figured out how sophistiratchet I am!

Eventually, I moved past my disdain for his friend and stopped giving her a major side eye, but she needed to fully understand that I wasn't up for those games. That was the first and last time that any woman would be stressing my husband out. Listen chick, don't demand anything from him that I don't even ask for, even it is for me. #ThanksForUnderstanding

IT'S ON GOD'S DESK

An acquaintance once approached me with a project idea. Because of the turmoil that I endured in 2015 when I did everything that I wanted to do and none of what God told me to do, I was adamant about checking with Him first. This time around, I truly prayed and asked God if that was a just a good move or if it was a God move. Not that there's anything wrong with her as a person. I love her! I truly do. But I was at a point where I felt like anything I did had to be God-led. I had already gone into business with friends previously without seeking God first and those ventures ended. They didn't end on a bad note, but I could've saved some time and money on both occasions. **#GPMUOG** – Make sure your actions are always God-led; Anything that costs you time or money needs to be run across God's desk before a final decision is made.

Interestingly enough, we attempted to make something happen and in the early stages, my spirit was uneasy. I knew that was a tell-tale sign that God was saying no. I was bummed about it too because we had an amazing idea that could have positively impacted people and their businesses. **#GPMUOG** – Every good idea is not a God idea! If you don't have peace about it, you don't need a piece of it.

Game From

The Culture

ALMOST MISSED MY NEXT

Thinking about how I almost missed my next still has me shaking my head in disbelief to this day. Because I made a careless decision about timing, I almost missed my next. No, it wasn't my next opportunity. It wasn't my next job or next boyfriend. Nor was it my next speaking engagement or writing gig. It wasn't even the next bus! Chile, I almost missed Next! You do know Next, right? *Baby, when we're grinding, I get so excited...* Yea, that Next!

It was 1998 and I had a severe case of senioritis. (This sounds like one of those stories that your grandma used to narrate, about when she used to walk five miles each way to school and back!) No, seriously. It was my last year of high school and, as a senior, you can probably imagine how I felt about that place. I could not wait to turn my tassel and toss my cap toward the clouds. There was one silver, glistening line in those clouds of high school and that was our open campus lunch privileges. Every day when that 6th-period bell rang, my lunch crew and I would roam the streets of Hyde Park looking for something to grub on. I still don't understand why on earth they allowed us to have open campus lunch. The only conclusion that I mustered up is that the local businesses had a hand in the decision making. Unfortunately, money usually speaks louder than sense, even when safety is jeopardized. I am still alive though, so I guess all was well.

That day I was out to lunch with one of my

homegirls. I don't remember where we were, but I will assume it was Pizza Hut. We used to love to hang out there because they had a jukebox. She would always put on *Thoughts of You* by Changing Faces. We were the only two people in the entire restaurant who had even heard of that jam. I still love that song to this day. ***I'm having these thoughts of you and I don't know what to do... #KPYUOG –*** After you find out how I almost missed my next, go listen to it. I can't just put you up on good game and not good music too!

Okay, okay. Back to the story...We both decided that we were not going to return to our 7th-period class, which was some business elective course that neither of us was taking seriously. After realizing that the 7th-period lunch was lame, we figured there was no use in getting an unexcused absence for class. We grabbed our pizza leftovers and drinks and headed back to the school. After trudging up three flights of stairs to our class, we found no one there. As a matter of fact, the entire 3rd floor was vacant. We were frantically running through the halls and pushing open every door looking for any sign of life. The scene eerily resembled a bad horror flick with Twilight Zone theme music in the blasting in the background. And you know what happens to the Black people in those horror films.

After combing the 3rd floor, we raced down a flight of stairs to do the same investigation on the 2nd floor. Still nothing. We were laughing, but I am sure nothing was funny. My heart was pounding in my chest. Was school over? Did everyone get an early dismissal? Was there an emergency? Dang, I gotta explain this to my mama! Just when I was about to start conjuring up my lie, an administrator bumped into us in the hall. Out of breath, we both screamed, "Where is everyone?"

"Oh, they're in the auditorium for the concert." We locked eyes with each other and shot off running toward our next. Truthfully, we didn't know who was on that stage, but we knew that we almost missed whatever surprise treat the school was handing out that day. Once we made it to the auditorium, panting and all, we waltzed right up to the stage like we knew that we belonged there. We danced, sang and even hopped on stage. *Step back, you're dancing kinda close. I feel a little poke coming through on you. (Next, Too Close)* Wait. Pause. Now that I am a full adult with girls of my own, I have a question! Why on earth was Next singing that song at a high school?!

Anywho, don't let me make you miss this next good game. **#GPMUOG** – Not being in position where you are called to be can cause you to miss your next. For you it may be your next big opportunity. Always stay in position so that God can find you doing what you are supposed to be doing when He comes looking to bless you. Let that soak in and then go back and listen to that Changing Faces song. It will bless you too!

EYEBROWS (NOT) POPPING

Oh Em Gee! A perfectly shaped eyebrow is sometimes more coveted by a woman than a fine man who is emotionally and physically available.

Okay, maybe we don't want great brows that much, but we do care immensely about them. Why can such a small patch of hair have such a huge impact on your entire face? You know when you find that one who can keep your brows on fleek or lit (or whatever word is hot now), you roll with them forever...or until she bounces on you like a gypsy in the night! And to think, you were so loyal to her! Oh, Carolyn, how I miss thee! You had truly figured my brows out.

Carolyn was my old brow guru who moved to Arizona several years back. Once she left me, I was hopping in and out of people's chairs like I had hotcakes in my pants. Yes, I was extremely brow artist promiscuous because I was looking to fill a void left by Carolyn. **#GPMUOG** – Most times when women are being promiscuous, they are seeking to fill a void.

With a gaping hole in my heart and maybe even a few holes in my eyebrows, I was on a quest to find a dope brow artist. Here is a glimpse into my journey of trying to find the magic lady.

1) Brow Girl #1 did a decent job, but I just never really felt like she appreciated my money. That was a huge problem for me because I work too hard for my coins.

2) Brow Girl #2 did an amazing job! She was the best thing since sliced Carolyn! The only problem was that she was just too far away.

3) Brow Girl #3 was such a sweet and gentle spirit. However, her work was just mediocre. She wasn't adding any pizzazz to my brows.

4) Brow Girl #4 did a great job and her personality

was stellar. We were working out great until…
5)   Brow Girl #5 came on the scene. She was really Brow Girl #2, but only this time she was so much closer!

I am sure everyone who has ever done my eyebrows is trying to figure out which one of these Brow Girls defines them. Girl, it doesn't even matter! All five of these girls can use this good game. **#GPMUOG** – If you are running a business, you must value your customer, have a reachable brand and be exceptional at your craft. There is no room for mediocrity when you are trying to sustain a company for the long haul.

LOVE & ~~HIP HOP~~ MARRIAGE

One of the greatest pieces of information that I have garnered was from Mona Scott-Young. Now, I'll have to come clean and admit that I pre-judged her based on the reputation of the reality shows that she executive produces. But honey, I saw her on a talk show and she spoke to how she's a top boss in the world, but once she enters her home she lets her man lead. I almost instantaneously put on my Team Mona shirt! That chick is cold, and I listen to cold chicks! Mona said she goes home and keeps her man happy because when he's happy, she's straight and then she can go out and really shut down the business game. Any woman in business who has a family needed to hear that! **#GPMUOG** – Don't ever be too prideful to take lessons from chicks that are doing what you want to be doing. You can learn something useful to your life from every single person walking this earth. Don't miss an enlightening moment because you have judged someone by how they look or even how they act. The key is to learn how to chew the meat and spit out the bones!

I'M JUDGING YOUR PLAY

When I first started working on this book, Luvvie Ajayi (whom I absolutely adore) was introducing the world to her book, *I'm Judging You*. I was so intrigued with how she was rolling it out. She gave advance copies to the media and celebrities and she could do that because she was well connected. Luvvie had the connections and network because she put in the work to get them. Even those that fell into her lap were a result of some work that she had done at some point in time. I mean, she was making regular appearances at the White House and I had yet to even get on the lawn! So, although I really admired how she was doing her thang, I couldn't do my thang like her thang. However, I needed to devise somethang that was going to be conducive to the deck of cards that I was working with. **#GPMUOG** –Stop getting all in your feelings because you don't have the resources (people, money, influence) that some people may have. God has provided you with everything that you need to get to the next level of life. Once you advance to that next level, He will have to make new provisions but, in the meantime, ***"work what you got"*** in my best Mary J. Blige voice! Make your next play your best play, even with the cards that you have been dealt.

79

A few short months later after she announced her new book, I was facilitating a workshop at a conference where Luvvie was the keynote speaker. (Wait, I just realized that I stood and presented on the same stage as Luvvie. **#GPMUOG** – We don't even realize that many times we are much further along than we give ourselves credit for.) As she was putting the finishing touches on her speech, she grabbed a seat in the foyer right next to me. It was just the two of us and I didn't say one word to her. Disappointed and angry with myself doesn't even begin to explain how I felt in the moments after my opportunity slipped away. Thankfully, all hope wasn't lost because later in the afternoon we were in very close proximity and I got a second chance to redeem myself. Only I didn't. I froze again. Afraid of looking too thirsty, I decided to say nothing. **#GPMUOG** – Concerning yourself with what other people think about you will allow opportunities of a lifetime to slip right through your index and middle fingers.

WRITERS READ

One of the most impactful books that I ever stuck my nose in is Charlamagne tha God's book, *Black Privilege*. That book literally changed my life! (He will be so happy to know that I spelled his name right!) **#KPYUOG** – Spelling people's names right is so important! How do you misspell someone's name and they sent you an email with the correct spelling? #HowSway? How?!

I recommend that you read his book when you

can make time. His story has the power to catapult you closer to your own destiny. I almost want to go to Moncks Corner and get my entire life together! I know the deep saints probably don't like Charlamagne because he calls himself "Tha God" and I get it. But, those people will miss out on some of the most golden nuggets of wisdom because they haven't mastered how to chew the meat and spit out the bones. **#GPMUOG** – There is valuable information to be gleaned from every person who walks this earth, even if you only take away what not to do. You need to learn how to sift out what is applicable and relevant to your life and toss away the rest. Sometimes the meat may be bones to you too. Just because something is right, doesn't mean that it is right for you. I don't eat chicken thighs, so even if you are serving up the meat, I am spitting that ish out like it's bones! #EverythingAintForEverybody Similarly, don't be too hasty and trash what you may think is bones. It could just be that your teeth haven't matured enough to break down the meat, so you confuse it with bones. In those cases, tuck the information safely away and watch God bring it to your remembrance when you need it the most.

Black Privilege inspired me in a way that I didn't expect it to. After reading that book, I commenced to giving zero you know whats about what anyone thought of Kristen. For the first time in my life, I was completely free of worrying about if people were going to think I was too much or extremely extra. I no longer cared if the questions, "Who does she think she is to do that?" or "Why does she dream so big?" came up. I was too busy being unapologetically me! Remember, no one wins when you don't show up and be everything that God called you to be. So, thank you Charlamagne for penning that book. You helped me inch that much closer to everything that God has laid up for me. I can't wait to share my story on your show!

I am really big fan of memoirs and autobiographies, so it is not uncommon to find me clad in a pair of colorful fuzzy socks, snuggled under a fleece blanket, reading an intriguing rags to riches story. That is why most of my favorite books are firsthand accounts. True writers read often, and I am no different. Listed below are more books that have had the greatest impact on me in recent years.

Year of Yes, Shonda Rhimes – Year of Yes taught me to never stifle my creativity or my children's either, for that matter.

Around the Way Girl, Taraji P. Henson – Now you already know how I feel about my girl T! Her memoir only made me love her more. I closed that book knowing that everything that I needed to succeed was already on the inside of me.

The Last Black Unicorn, Tiffany Haddish – I didn't know whether to belt out a gut-busting laugh or drop my jaw in utter shock while reading this book. However, what I did know was that Tiffany has been through some serious ish. Life has truly dealt her some blows and her story is proof that the greater your struggles, the greater your successes. Her witty stories inspired me beyond explanation.

Girl Boss, Sophia Amoruso – This book reminded me that my dreams are valid. In the most hilarious way, Sophia was able to inspire me to keep on pushing hard for my visions to manifest to reality. *Girl Boss* was the truth! Reading that book led me to later watching the *Girl Boss* series on Netflix. The way that series changed my life in June of 2017... Maybe I will discuss that later too.

Draw the Circle, Mark Batterson – *Draw the Circle* shifted my prayer life into a new dimension. After completing the 40-day prayer challenge in the book, I realized how small I had been playing it with my prayers. My prayers became bigger, more focused and more frequent.

Of course, as an avid reader, there are other stories that have positively impacted me including *30-Day Stay* by Tiffany Huff and *Self-Made* by Nely Galan. I would be remiss not to mention the Holy Bible because much of my inspiration, correction, and motivation comes from that book. I just don't always stop there. Christians often get so deep that we think the only place that we can find inspiration is in the Bible. **#GPMUOG** – God is everywhere, and He can send you a word however He chooses. Be receptive to the game whenever it arrives!

Game From

The Hill

WIFEY IS WIFE-LIKE

When I was around 17 years old, I began my relationship with Jake, who would eventually become my first love and the first man to shatter my heart into pieces. Jake and I were together for almost four years and no one could have paid me a gazillion dollars to convince me that we were not going to get married. We had an amazing connection, which fostered a powerful coupleship. Of course, we had small disagreements here and there, but overall life was beautiful for us together.

It was so beautiful that we moved in together during my second year of college. My parents dropped me off at my dorm room in August, helped me move in and by the time they were heading northbound on I-65 back to Chicago, Jake and I were moving my belongings out of the dormitory. In the blink of an eye, I went from a girl with a boyfriend to a woman living with a man. Up until that point, I was a straight A college student, so I had to work hard to maintain that level of excellence. I had the fear of God in me via my Clutch Girl and I wasn't going to dare let my grades slip and then she would have to find out that I was living with that dude. I probably would not even be here to share this story!

Living with Jake meant that I was going to school, grocery shopping, cooking meals, helping to pay bills, and keeping a house. Of course, as a shacking couple, I was sexing him too. When Jake realized all that I was putting into our relationship, he started calling me Wifey. Yes, "Wifey" like the song. Clearly, the group Next was an integral part of my

young adult life! Wifey. I proudly smiled every time
he said it. Hearing him call me Wifey made my
heart pitter patter in a way that I had never
experienced before. Unfortunately, that pitter-patter
would soon transition to more of a shattering glass
sound as he began to break my heart.

One evening in early May, only by an act of God,
Wifey caught Jake amid his plot to sleep with the
girl who lived downstairs. Aimee lived directly
under us; I mean she could have heard Jake having
sex with me! At this time, I was living between the
apartment that I shared with Jake and my dorm
room. It is a long story how I ended up with another
dorm room for the second semester, but I'll sum it
up by saying that staying on campus was much
more convenient for me. I cannot reiterate enough
how important it was for me to make it to class and
maintain my high grade point average!

That evening, I was in my dorm room waiting for
Jake to pick me up and take me to my second home.
I was seriously craving a 3-piece tender with red
beans and rice from Popeyes and Jake, who was
quite accommodating, was on his way to get it for
me. Then, after he got the chicken, he would be over
to scoop me up. He called my room phone to let me
know that he would be downstairs in the back of the
dorm in 20 minutes. As I started gathering my
homework and packing my overnight bag, the
phone rang again.
"Hello."
No answer.
"Hello."
Silence again.

"He-loooooo?"
Still nothing.

I was gripping my cordless phone in my right hand with my thumb just about to depress the phone button to hang up when something stopped me dead in my tracks. That something was probably a little bit of women's intuition and a whole lot of nosey. Either way, I see it as God putting me up on game because He gifted me the intuition and nosiness is a trait that has been passed through generations of women in my family. So, He had His hand in that one too!

As I listened intently with the phone muted, I heard Jake telling his boy how he planned to pick me up and spend just enough quality time with me to appease me. "You know she has a dorm room now. So, I am going to drop her back off at her room and then go home to f^$% with Aimee." To this day I am not completely sure the word *with* was even in his statement but to me it didn't even matter. Immediately, I called upstairs to my girl Domini, who is still my good sister-friend to this day, because she had a car and could drive me over to the house. In less than five minutes, we had rallied the troops and our little girl gang piled into Domini's blue '85 Toyota Camry. The whole ride over to the apartment, I was fuming.

How could he do this to me? I am Wifey! As soon as I get to this house, I am trashing all of his ish! I am moving out! I hate this nigga! But I love him so much.

Tears.
Real tears.
Heavy, exasperated breathing.
Heart palpitations.
More tears.

By the time we made it to the Pinehurst Apartments, I was ready to fight but I knew the fight would not be with Jake. After all, he was probably downstairs in the back of the dorm repeatedly calling my room. Since he wasn't home, I decided the next best person to battle was Aimee. Domini hadn't even stopped the car, but I had already hopped out and was banging on Aimee's door. "I know you're in there!" I was yelling so loudly that the neighbors were starting to peek through their blinds. Clearly, delirium had set in because Aimee's burnt orange Mitsubishi Eclipse wasn't even in her parking space. "She's not home Krissy. C'mon, let's get your stuff." My girl Keshia was firm, yet compassionate in her directives as she gently nudged me up the steps.

Once inside, my girls quickly got in formation as if we had rehearsed the game plan on the way over there. We had an assembly line going as I passed them anything that I felt I needed to take and that would fit in the car ride back. During this process, something clicked, and I remembered the birthday cake that I just purchased Jake a couple of days prior. In a manic rage, I ran to the refrigerator, yanked the cake out and grabbed the first butcher knife I could locate. I started stabbing the cake like it was the one who had me believing that I was Wifey.

For a moment in time, I think I did black out and imagine that I was stabbing Jake. Thank God for that cake because I could possibly still be serving time for really hurting that man. At some point during my fit of rage, Jake entered the apartment to find me stabbing his birthday cake and my friends looking at him like, "Umm hmm.. She caught you."

As any man would do, he pulled me in the room away from my friends and tried to explain. But there was no need for an explanation. He had spoken the words from his mouth and my ears had grabbed every single one. Our amazing coupleship was over. I was no longer Wifey and just like that, I pushed past Jake and told my girls that it was time to go. The ride back to the yard was eerily silent. I would love to tell you that that was the absolute end of us, but I told you that I don't lie. I'll share more about Jake another time, maybe even in another book. For now, he has already taken up too much real estate in this book!

I never let another man who was not my husband call me wifey, wife or anything of the like again. When you let a man call you "wifey" or wife and you're not married, it's not only disrespectful to you but it's disrespectful to the sanctity of marriage. Real wives will tell you that you haven't yet experienced the work, the warfare or the wherewithal that comes with changing your last name. So, stop letting him call you that if he hasn't done anything to solidify the deal. I know you think it's cute and endearing, but it's not. It's insulting to you because he's just dangling a carrot in your face to keep you along for the ride. Tell him to dangle some carats instead.

It is time to quit playing house and pretend wife. You are a grown woman who knows what she really wants out of life and if you keep playing house, you will always be a pretend wife. So, stop pretending that you don't desire to be a real wife and not just wifey or wife-like or the one who does everything a wife should do but never gets the benefits of formally being his wife.

#GPMUOG – If you continue to allow him to treat you like a fake wife, all while performing real wife duties, he will be comfortable with the way that things are. Furthermore, if he has not pledged to make you a real wife, don't be surprised when he commits fake adultery. People, including men, will only treat you the way you allow. One of the most important skills that you must master is training others how they should conduct themselves when dealing with you.

MEET DIME BONE

Well the time has finally come for your formal introduction to Dime Bone aka Dime Bizzle or if you want to go all the way in, Dime Bizzle off the Hizzle for Shizzle my Nizzle. I just closed my eyes, threw my head back and let out a hearty laugh on that one! Dime Bone used to be the ish! Well, she still is the ish but she just carries that ish much differently these days.

Dime Bone was born sometime during late 2000 when her and her best friend at the time, Dime Plush, were simply carrying out their normal antics of extraness. Because they both were self-proclaimed dime pieces, they created these aliases so that people could speak that ten-piece anointing over their lives daily. I just chuckled out loud again! Dime Bone chose her name because although she was hardly a light-skinned chick, she especially loved to hear girls affirm themselves as "red bones." Secretly, she longed to be a bone too but "brown bone" or "caramel bone" just didn't have the same finesse as her lighter counterparts. Her joyful remedy finally came when she and Plush decided to create their new monikers.

Although Dime Bone was officially born somewhere in Chicago, probably on the way to the club while the body that she occupied was smoking weed (because she got creative when she was "blowing"), she truly blossomed into the fullness of who she was destined to be on the campus of Alabama A&M University. If you were to survey 100 people who were students on the Hill during the years of 1999-2003, I would bet that at least 70% know or have at least heard of Dime Bone. She was really the ish!

That girl never wanted to be or look like anyone else. So much so that anytime there was a major event going on – and at an HBCU there is *always* a major event going on – you could find her on the floor of her bedroom with a pair of scissors in her hand, cutting and creating the most unusual outfit. Dime Bone couldn't sew if her life depended on it. Heck, she could barely thread a needle! Yet, she created amazingly unique garments and all she needed was her scissors, hot glue gun, and random embellishments that she found around her apartment.

D. Bone, as Guy Z (her beau at the time) nicknamed her, was charismatic, energetic, and the life of the party! She was incredibly fun, extremely flirty and a bit feisty. All the men wanted to be with her and all the women wanted to befriend her. When both couldn't quite figure out a way to do so, they opted to strongly dislike her. But Dime Bone did not care; her life was the epitome of carefreeness. She gave zero you know whats. D. Bone was especially determined too. It did not matter who or what was between where she was and what she wanted. That chick would go ferociously plowing through any obstacles that stood in her way as if she was a professional wide receiver. There was little, if any, thought given to the feelings, egos or relationships that would be crushed along the way.

One of the most well-rounded females that I know, Dime Bone could adapt to any group of people. After all, she had grown up with the most racist of white people and hung with the most hood of Black folks during her elementary and high school years. So, college was truly no different. She was a sorority girl, so she knew all the Greeks on campus. Dime Bone was exceptionally smart, at one point maintaining a 3.9 grade point average as a civil engineering major. Hanging out with the smart kids that most deemed as nerds was natural to her because she was so intelligent, but her street side longed to be fed as well. Thus, D. Bone knew all the ones that society would label as misfits and roughnecks by name too. After her classes were done each day, you could probably find her chilling somewhere, smoking a blunt and having an impromptu freestyle rap battle with her family. Her family was mostly guys who were committed to looking out for her. There was a cousin, a special friend, and a host of others who just took care of Dime Bone the best way they knew how. I am convinced that most of them secretly wanted more from her and she may have even given it to them. Nevertheless, she loved every one of them like they were her blood and knew that she could count on them to hold her down.

Even with all her partying and kicking it, one thing remained consistent. Dime Bone took care of her business and she did not play about her grades. Dime Bone was very clear on her assignment at Alabama A&M; she had only come with the intentions of leaving with a degree. Otherwise, she would have stayed at home and run the mean streets of Chicago. There definitely was no need to journey down to the dirty south if she wasn't going to graduate.

If Dime Bone were to look back on her antics today, she would immediately recognize how much she has grown over the last seventeen years. I am sure that she would want to apologize to all the people that she intentionally hurt as she fought for what she believed belonged to her. Instead of working to tear women down, she would be fighting to build them up. Dime Bone would be sharing her story so that others could get free.

I am sure that she is remorseful, apologetic, and

has grown tremendously. I know these things to be true because – well – if your mind processors run just a little slow, I am Dime Bone. She is I and I am her! Dime Bone was such a force to be reckoned with that I must speak of her in third person! Many of the things that comprised Dime Bone's makeup are the same things that I am today. I am still that cool homegirl that can hang out with my girls and chill with the fellas. Only now, the fellas usually mean my husband and his crew. My intelligence and over the top personality are still here. Well, most of it. Today, I am not a person who steps on others to get what I want. I have grown to be very sensitive to the feelings of others, often taking them into more consideration than my own well-being.

Dime Bone revealed one distinct characteristic to me though. She proved just how much influence God had given me. Without social media or a marketing campaign or a podcast appearance or anything else that would have given me instant, widespread recognition, I convinced a campus full of my peers that Kristen R. Love's name was really Dime Bone. People were literally calling me Dime Bone. Imagine being 100 feet away from someone and hearing them yell, "What's Up Dime Bone?!" Let that marinate. Dime. Bone. One would've thought that my birth certificate read Dime R. Bone, born on November 24, 1980. But it didn't, and I got them to buy into my outrageousness simply because God had gifted me with some powerful influence. **#GPMUOG** – When God has blessed you with the gift of influence, you have a choice to either use it to motivate the masses to nothingness, evil practices or something for your own selfish gain. Or you can opt to exercise your influence responsibly and promote productivity, positivity, and point everything back to the one who can take credit for it all – God. Everything in you can be used by God for His purposes but you must be open to the cleansing process. When you accept Jesus as your Lord and Savior, His blood washes you, but the next step after that and the next step after that and so on is to get up and allow the Holy Spirit to change you.

GOD ALWAYS COMES THROUGH IN A CLUTCH

Dime Bizzle knew God and she loved Him greatly. She understood His love for her to the limits of her mental capacity. The way God provided for her, even when she was undeserving, was always appreciated. There was this one time when she was literally homeless with no money. Now when I say homeless, it wasn't lying on the street atop a flattened cardboard with everything she owned scattered around creating a makeshift fortress of protection type of homeless. God came through with provisions like only He can before her circumstances had an opportunity to make a turn for that level of homelessness.

As the summer of 2002 ended and D. Bone was at the beginning of the very last year of her college matriculation, she found herself sleeping from pillar to post every night. Lucky for her, she had a host of accommodating friends who didn't mind her crashing on their couches. Careful not to exasperate her welcome at any one spot, she only spent a maximum of two nights in the same place before hitting the next apartment in her rotation. With no money, no plan, and no options, Dime Bone was working hard to resist switching into panic mode, but it was becoming increasingly difficult to keep panic at bay. After about two weeks of that nomad wandering and classes set to start in just a few days, she found herself desperate for a miracle. I have already stressed to you how important school was to the girl and she was not about to get to her last semester and destroy what she had purposefully built. There were no answers in plain sight and her hope was diminishing rapidly. In that moment, D. Bone prayed the most simplistic, yet profound prayer that she had probably ever parted her lips to whisper. "God, I need You. I need a miracle." Dime Bone relied on that breath prayer and the tiny sliver of faith that she had left to trust that God heard her and that He was going to answer. At that moment her faith was small, but it produced big results.

#GPMUOG – "I tell you the truth, if you had faith even as small as a mustard seed, you could say to this mountain, 'Move from here to there,' and it would move. Nothing would be impossible." Matthew 17:20 NLT

Two days later Dime Bizzle was pleasantly surprised to get a call from one of her grandmothers in the early evening hours.

"Hello."

"Hey, Kristina." (Her grandma didn't call her Dime Bone. She preferred her special nickname of Kristina.)

"Hi, Grandma! How are you?"

"Oh, I am doing okay. How are you, baby?"

"Well," Dime Bone let out a loud exaggerated sighed, "I am doing okay Grandma."

"You don't sound okay."

"I am really trying to be. That new roommate situation didn't work out and I was forced to abruptly vacate the apartment. Grandma, I don't have anywhere to stay, I don't have any money and my classes are about to start. I am starting to stress because I don't know what to do."

"All you need to be worrying about is finishing school. Tomorrow I want you to find an apartment and call me back and let me know how much money you need to get it."

Knowing that her grandma was making it on a fixed income and fully aware of the costs required to secure an apartment, Dime Bone initially declined. "Grandma, that is okay. I will figure it out."

#GPMUOG – When God sends the answer to your prayer, don't reject it. Let God bless you. When He sends someone to be the vessel to bless you, don't reject them. Let God bless them for being a blessing to you.

"Listen. Do what I said and call me back tomorrow."

"Okay, Grandma. Thank you. I love you."

"I love you too baby."

D. Bone did exactly as her grandmother instructed and well before she slipped into a deep sleep on her line sister's couch the next night, she had keys to her new apartment in her purse. Reflecting on the transpiration of events that led to that moment, Dime Bizzle was in awe of the miracle that God had performed in her life. She knew that her grandmother loved her endlessly and was praying for her while she was away at school, but it was not customary for the matriarch of her family to just call her out of the blue. Yet, Dime Bone knew that it was not really out of the blue. God quickened her spirit with an unction to check on her Kristina. Grandma already knew that her grandbaby needed her before any hellos were exchanged. Her Kristina was grateful that her Grandma was a willing vessel for a clutch blessing.

GOD PUTS THE CHERRY ON TOP

Within two days of speaking to her grandmother, Dime Bone was all moved into her apartment. And by being all moved in, I mean that she solicited the help of one of her girlfriends to pack up their car with her clothes and dishes and transport them to her new address. Feelings of gratefulness, excitement, and relief were soon replaced with more anxiety, worry, and fear of the unknown as she stood in the dining area of a naked apartment. The girl didn't have a single piece of furniture to fill the place. Dorm room. Boyfriend's apartment. Dorm room. Furnished campus apartment. Failed roommate's apartment. Every place that Dime Bone had previously lived came with the convenience of being fully furnished. She was a bit discouraged thinking about how she was going to hurdle that mountain, yet that wasn't even hardly D. Bizzle's biggest issue.

Her apartment was over 5 miles away from the campus and ever since she had to bury her first "son" Stanley, she had been hitchhiking with anyone who had enough pity on her to provide a ride. However, that was not a feasible and dependable plan with her new living arrangement. By now, I am certain you understand how important school was to D. Bone. She had to get to class and she needed to have reliable transportation to do so. What was just perceived as a blessing began to look more like the complete opposite. Thoughts that could only be sponsored by hell started to dance through her mind.

See? I should have just told Grandma no. I don't even have furniture for this place. I have no way to get back and forth to class. This apartment is more of a hurt than a help. I should have just continued to sleep on friends' couches.

#GPMUOG – When God sends your miracle, don't let the devil make you second guess it. If God has made a miraculous provision in your circumstances, trust that He will also provide a way for you to maintain the blessing.

I cannot recall if Dime Bone prayed for another miracle or if she continued to wallow in her sorrows but either way, God came through in the clutch again and put a huge cherry on top. Dime Bone had been the recipient of a major scholarship award for the previous three years. The scholarship was funded by a foundation headed by one of the wealthiest couples in the world. Each semester, a disbursement check was sent directly to the school to cover D. Bone's financial obligations in full. For whatever reason (read an act of God), that final year of school, they opted to switch the process. With classes beginning in just 2 days, she received another unexpected phone call. That time the voice on the other end was not one that she recognized.

"Hello."
"Hi, may I speak with Kristen Love?"
"This is she."
"Hi, Kristen." (I am pretty sure that none of her records had Dime Bone listed as a point of contact.) "I am Molly from _____ and I am calling to get a mailing address where you can receive an overnight package. We would like to mail your tuition check directly to you this semester."

"Uh, give me a second. I just moved here, and I don't know my address yet," she said with a laugh indicating that she was slightly embarrassed.

Dime Bone immediately recognized that phone call as God sending her just what she needed precisely when she needed it. With only two classes left until she fulfilled her graduation requirements, she knew that her check was going to be more than enough to sustain her. At the peak of her heightened anticipation, the FedEx guy knocked on her the door at her new address with an envelope delivery. The guy was barely back to his truck before she had a grabbed the tab and ripped the envelope open. Alas! In her hand, she held the ticket to erase most of her fears and issues for at least a few months. The check was for over $10,000!

By the time she was resting comfortably in her seat on the first day of class, Dime Bone had furnished her entire pad. It was swanky too; she was thoroughly impressed with her contemporary, *MTV Cribs* vibe. Additionally, she drove her new car to the yard that Tuesday morning. She was able to purchase a 1996 Pontiac Grand Am. Her newest baby was green in complexion and one of her beloved line sisters befittingly named him Lil' Money.

As the professor was reviewing the syllabus, D. Bone's mind drifted into a prayer of thanksgiving. In a matter of days, You have shifted my entire situation. Thank You for sending me a miracle. Thank You for always coming through in a clutch. Thank You for adding a few cherries to the top this time! I love You so!
#GPMUOG – God is able to do immeasurably more than all you can ask or imagine. (Ephesians 3:20) He can do it suddenly too!

LEAVE WELL ENOUGH ALONE

When women cut their hair, either something major just happened or is about to happen. It could be a milestone birthday, a major weight loss or just a reinvention of self. For so many of us, it has a lot to do with a man. This is especially true after a breakup. Three weeks after one of the biggest blow-ups with Guy Z, I went and chopped all my hair off. We had finally ended our tumultuous "relationship" and I was ready to release any dead weight that was attached to Z. Shana, one of the best stylists to have ever blessed my crown, cut the sexiest little pixie style and you could not tell me that Dime Bone was not popping! Later that evening I headed out to one of the local clubs to hang out with my girls. Of course, I would love to say that it was all about spending some much needed time catching up with the ladies, but in the depths of my soul, I knew that Z would be there. I recall that I didn't too much care for my glasses with my new cut and I was fresh out of contacts, so I opted to just be visually impaired for the entire night. I know it was foolish, but I had to be fly baby!

The girls and I were having a meeting in the bathroom. *I've got a meeting in the ladies room. I'll be back real soon. (Klymaxx, Meeting in the Ladies Room)* As we were readying to exit, one of my favorite girls ran back in and excitedly whispered, "He's out there Krissy." There I was, blind as a bat, but finer than May wine! I boldly walked out of that restroom and acted as if I didn't see him because I really couldn't! My crew told me that he did a double take as I walked by and of course before the night got started good, he came to find me. The off was then on again. I really wished I would have tapped into my arsenal of God game at that precise moment because I would have never gotten back involved in that situation. **#GPMUOG** –

When God removes something or someone from your life, leave well enough alone! Don't go to pick it or them back up.

YOU WERE BORN TO WIN

Finding myself on the receiving end of sucky relationships that ended with me bawling my eyes out because things didn't work out as I expected automatically certified me as the expert of broken hearts and failed relationships. Thus, it was only appropriate that I founded the entire *I'm The One That Got Away* ™ movement. With Ashanti's *Foolish* – **See my days are cold without you, but I'm hurting while I'm with you** – on repeat in my dorm room and on my voicemail intro, it was evident to everyone both near and far that I was going through my first major heartbreak with Jake. If I keep it as 100 as I have this entire time, then I have to admit that the pain that I experienced from Jake was a payment that was due to me. The check had been written as early as 1996 when I dumped my then boyfriend without so much as an explanation. I turned around and did the exact thing in 1998 when I gave my prom date the ax because I wanted to pursue my relationship with Jake. So, all that heart-wrenching pain that I attributed to Jake was also some fault of my own. Don't get me wrong; I absolutely blame him for the way that his lying, cheating and selfish ways drove a wedge between us. But that chick Karma is a real you know what and she always makes good on her IOUs. She will come to administer what rightfully belongs to you.

#GPMUOG – Do not be deceived. God cannot be mocked. A (wo) man reaps what (s)he sows. Galatians 6:7 NIV

I imagine that each of my exes who took notice of the #ITOTGA movement probably wanted to give me an earful about how into myself I am, but deep down they knew that I was telling the truth. If I was a man, I would want a woman just like me and I am not saying that because it's me! To have a chick that you can chill with and chat with like the boys and then have that same chick turn around and be the — well you already know enough about me by now to finish painting the picture.

I wasted so much time giving my all to men who were not committed to learning how to reciprocate those gifts. There I was thinking that I was winning because I had good-looking men who loved to flaunt me around because I was fine too but what I desired the most was much deeper than our appearances. I wanted them to pray for me and pray for us like I was praying for us. Being considered first seemed like something so basic, yet all the guys that I was dealing with acted like I was asking them to do Chinese math at a rap concert, surrounded by ten thousand screaming fans. My version of winning was really a hand of no spades. Losing.

If you're losing (and by losing, I mean that you are allowing a man to treat you like crap), something is gravely wrong. Both of you are discounting your value. You are so powerful beyond nature. You were fashioned from a rib. Do you understand that the very essence, the core of who you are, is a rib? The rib cage protects the heart and lungs. That must be an extraordinarily strong structure to be tasked with guarding two of the most important organs in the human body. Baby, it gets no stronger than that!

So yes, you are a being of amazing strength and you have supreme power. Why are you letting someone who doesn't understand that power belittle and disrespect you? Somewhere, at this exact moment, there is a man wondering how to get to you. He is willing to learn how to love you in every way imaginable. You're different and special in every way imaginable. *You love me from my hair follicle to my toenails. (Jill Scott, He Loves Me)* That feels so good too, especially after you've experienced everything else that wasn't that. **#GPMUOG** – He has someone just for you, but if you have someone in the spot that doesn't belong, you hold up the process.

If you recall, I had my first encounter meeting with my husband in August of 2002. My birthday fell on a Sunday a few short months later. To celebrate, I invited all my close girlfriends to worship with me at church. Right after my purchase of Lil' Money, I made sure to uphold my promise to God to start back going to church whenever He blessed me with a car. All the folks around me with cars would call me in a heartbeat to hit up the club and party, yet no one ever called on Sunday morning for me to accompany them to church. **#GPMUOG** – Although God uses people to bless others often, He doesn't need them to do so. If there are people who are not aiding you in getting you to your destiny, God will step over everyone just to bless you with what you need. No God Jrs needed! Just be sure to keep up your end of the bargain if you made a promise to Him!

Okay, back to my 22nd birthday! I can still see the day clearly, from the maroon crushed corduroy pants and coordinating sheer, floral top that I wore to the stirring sermon that day and especially the prophetic words spoken directly to me at the conclusion of the service. Out of nowhere a beautiful brown-skinned woman who I had seen before but knew nothing about approached me. I was admiring her fly haircut, but she was not concerned with anything of the flesh. That woman marched right up to me like she had been sent on a classified mission. She grabbed my chin in a way that said, "Look at me, girl. And listen." Ordinarily, I would've been on the defense and shot her some nasty look that responded with "Girl. And who the hell are you?!" like only D. Bone could. However, she had such a spirit of authority that I immediately straightened up and looked her square in the face. Even her words commanded attention as they dripped with authority.

"God said. To. Let. That. Man. Go. He has something better for you, but He can't give it you because you won't let that other man go. I don't know who He is talking about, but you do."

Before she could finish serving me my entire life on a silver platter, in the front of the church on my birthday, the tears were falling on my upper lip. She was right. I knew exactly what He was talking about. I had to let Z go because there was someone better. God wanted to give me my forever, but I was

stuck with what was supposed to be the past.
#GPMUOG – Sometimes we can be so madly in
love with people that we can't even see that they are
just a distraction from what God truly has for us.

In my mind, Z and I were going to be together
for the long haul. Looking back on that today, I can't
believe I was that stupid. He could have never been
the man that I needed for the woman that I am
today. Heck, he couldn't even be the man I needed
then, and I hadn't even started becoming the
woman that God had destined me to be!
#GPMUOG – When God blesses you with a mate,
he will be the person for where you are going, not
for where you are. Trust His process because you
don't know the plans. Stop losing in these
relationships, when God created you to win!

Game From

The Hustle

MY CANDLE BURNS FROM BOTH ENDS

There is almost never a moment in my life that I am not doing more than one thing at a time. If I am writing a book, I am simultaneously listening to a podcast to garner innovative information. While I am cooking dinner, I am catching up with a girlfriend who I normally may not have time to chat with. During the rare occasions that I have a minute to watch television, my time may be shared with combing the girls' hair or doubling as a date night with my hubby. I hardly ever find the chance to just be operating in a one-dimensional vein. Because I am constantly doing what many deem as "too much," I am often taunted by those who simply cannot understand the life that I live.

I have a friend who constantly repeats the phrase, "you can't burn a candle from both ends" to me. However, I just never really seemed to agree with that statement. The only way that I am going to be successful and be a great wife, mother, daughter, sister, friend, servant, businesswoman, speaker, teacher, writer, inspirer, and voice of empowerment to women around the globe is to burn the candle from both ends. At least that's going to have to be my life until I can afford to hire other people to relieve some of my load. I didn't necessarily explain that to her, but I didn't need to because she probably wouldn't have understood my scenario anyway. *Here we go yo, here we go yo. So what's the, what's the, what's the scenario? (A Tribe Called Quest, Scenario)* She wasn't living it. You do not have to try to explain your position to everyone, all the time. **#GPMUOG** – When you are in a predicament where you are working to get into a better position, you have to do what is within God's will to get there. No, many may not fully comprehend your level of commitment and sacrifice, but the ones who really love you will eventually come to a level of understanding and support.

Coincidentally (even though I have already told you that I don't believe in coincidence), a day after one of our conversations where she repeated that idiom to me, I was perusing Instagram and stumbled across a meme that read, "To succeed, you have to be willing to burn the candle at both ends." It was just what I needed to remind me that it is okay to be different. My friend and I live two remarkably different lives and it is not that one is more important or harder or better than the other. We just have strikingly unique circumstances and that means that how we handle situations is going to be very different. **#GPMOUG** – You need to be okay with being different. You must find contentment with people not understanding your choices. If you know that God is leading you on this journey, you have to find security in knowing that everything will be beautiful in the end.

GIVE YOUR GIFT AWAY

When I first released my book, *Queens Turn Pain Into Power*, I instantly started giving the story away to people. Not the entire book though, because I still wanted them to buy it. But I released just enough to intrigue them. (That is how you date too, by the way. Just enough to intrigue them. Men must be intrigued.) But anyway, I submitted my stuff to podcasts, for speaking gigs, blogs, radio shows, whatever! At first, I was talking myself out of it. "Girl, you haven't even arrived yet!" But then I snapped back, "Girl, you don't need to arrive yet. You have a story to tell, they want a story to share and the people want a story to hear!" We live in a digital age of reality television. Everyone wants to know what is going on in other people's lives. I decided to use that to my advantage. There was this one podcast that I absolutely loved. *Cool Soror* is hosted by Rashan Ali, a radio and television personality out of Atlanta. I fell in love with her podcast because she was interviewing members of Black Greek letter organizations who were willing to share their story with her listening audience. After combing my book for the juiciest excerpt, I sent it over to her. I talked myself in and out of it at least a dozen times before hitting send. Part of it was because the story that I was sharing was about my sexual assault as a child. But it was also because I was worried about what she would think or say when she opened the email of some random chick that she had never heard of. But I pushed pass those doubts and sent it anyway. I made it on her show a short time after that! I truly believe that it was all because I gave my gift away and I did it afraid. **#GPMUOG** – The best opportunities for your life are going to be well outside your comfort zone. You may be nervous and fearful about journeying beyond the parameters of your zone but do it afraid. But, never be afraid to share your gift freely with the world. What you give away always comes back with a greater return than you could have ever imagined. You cannot beat God's giving!

As I prepared for my Skype interview with Rashan, I petitioned God to find out exactly what He wanted me to share with the *Cool Soror* listeners. His response was simple, yet so complex. "Tell them to live their life on purpose. Urge her listeners to seek Me to find out why I created them and then wake up every single day and do what I tell them." Our interview ended with just that. **#GPMUOG** – Whenever you have the chance to influence and impact the masses, always seek God on what He wants you to share.

THE BIRTHING PLAN BIRTHED ME

February 27, 2016 – "I am a midwife. I help women discover they're PREGNANT with PURPOSE & then help them PUSH past their PAIN to DELIVER what God has PROMISED them!"

Those words are nestled somewhere safely between the kids' future birthday plans and my list of my gift wishes that I keep handy in the notes app on my phone in case anyone wants to bless me with a spontaneous gift. Just in case you want to know, my list is simple. New Pandora charms, hot pink Air Max (size 10), a bike, lifetime Delta dues, meal prepping service and a few other things. Don't hesitate to ask if you need to know where to send your kind gestures!

Seriously, when I first typed that statement about being a midwife, I had no idea what it even meant. I can't even tell you why I wrote it. I am inclined to believe that God was helping me begin to set His plans in motion. He is responsible for writing that vision statement for my life. In a moment when I was probably just messing around, He put me up on game concerning my purpose. I was not aware in February of 2016, but God was essentially spelling out for me why I was created. **#GPMUOG** – The two most important days of your life are the day that you're born and the day that you discover why. The why is an assignment, specifically designated for you, that will fill a void in the earth. Even if you aren't doing traditional ministry work, God will make a great use of you and everything that He has gifted you with.

It would be several months later before I would see anything tangible come to fruition behind those words that I saved on February 27, 2016. In September, I had the unction to start working on a curriculum for a program that I would later name The Birthing Plan. Still unaware of exactly what I was doing, I trudged ahead anyway, all at the leading of the Spirit. I had zero clues as to what I was doing. As I worked through completing the workbook for the program, the vision of me as

midwife finally began to materialize. **#GPMUOG** –
Often, God will give you a glimpse of what's to
come. Yet, it may be months, even years before you
see that vision beginning to take shape. Remain
patient. When He begins to reveal the action steps,
make the moves, even if you still don't understand
the process. In due time, all things will be revealed.

After starting and stopping numerous times and
waiting for more divine inspiration, I finally
finished the curriculum for The Birthing Plan in
November and I felt confident that I was about to
change women's lives! I was ready to secure my first
clients for the program that was set to start at the
beginning of 2017.

When I first introduced The Birthing Plan
Program, it had a price tag attached to it. Albeit, I
thought the price was very reasonable. However,
God changed those plans very quickly. At His
urging, I changed the price for the program to
free.99. To fully comprehend how ridiculous this
was, let me remind you that I was going to be
helping these women give birth! I was on board as
their midwife to help them push past all the junk
that had aborted their dreams and caused them to
miscarry in the past. Every midwife and doula I
know gets paid! I wanted to be in that number too.
At the end of the first cohort, the ladies had birthed
customer service and human resource consulting
companies, written & published devotionals, taken
their catering businesses to new heights, grown in
their confidence, garnered necessary business and
life skills and so much more. That's why I knew that
I should be getting paid, but God blocked it! I

couldn't understand why He would keep me from getting that money. After all, some of that cold hard green was already on the table. Did you read what I said? Somebody had money on the table! So, I was looking at the table with the money and then looking back up at God, thinking, "Do You really want me to leave these coins on the table? You KNOW I need this money!" **#GPMUOG –** "Anytime I redirect you from what you think you need, it is because I am sending you to something much better. However, understanding and accepting that takes a completely submitted will and a heart that truly trusts Me." Charlamagne tha God refers to this as divine misdirection in his book.

Hoping that I was hearing it all wrong or that God was going to have a change in His heart, all I had in response was a "say what, now?" Not only was it crazy but it was affecting my bottom line. To say that I was utterly confused by it all would be an understatement. But a dear friend reminded me that I wanted to be used by God. That I almost begged Him to use me. I wanted my life to be a vessel through which His light was carried to His daughters. I just thought it would feel differently. Warm and fuzzy on the inside is what I imagined being used by God feeling like. After all, GOD was using me! It doesn't get more honorable than that. So why was I feeling so conflicted, upset, and disappointed? **#GPMUOG –** When you say, "Use me, God," understand that the phrase comes with pain. Being used hurts! Whenever anyone uses you, it's uncomfortable, painful, angering, and sometimes lonely. The only difference is that when God uses you, He helps with the pain management and His benefits and blessings far exceed the pain.

After I made the announcement that The Birthing Plan was being sponsored by God and His team, I received a heap of phone calls. The decision seemed very drastic and extremely unpopular. Most of the callers wanted to let me know that I was making a terrible mistake. "I don't think this is a good idea, Kristen." To which I would honestly and sardonically retort, "Yea, I don't either, but I know what God said." Between those calls, came a few of a different nature. Those were from women who desperately wanted to enroll in the program but just couldn't afford The Birthing Plan before the price was changed. I especially recall one young lady's story. She dropped me a line to say thank you after hearing the great news.

"When I first saw the description of The Birthing Plan, I knew that I needed to be involved. I have been stagnant for so long and I know that you can help me. Although the registration fee was very reasonable for what we will be receiving, I just cannot afford it right now. But I prayed and asked God to make a way for me to attend because I really wanted it. Today, I opened my email to find that it was free. Even if He didn't, I feel like God did this just for me! So, thank You for being used."

All we can do is say yes to being used. We don't get to determine how He uses us.

BRANDING 101

Just like Whitney's real family and friends called her Nippy, people who really love and know me, call me Krissy. If you call me Krissy, then you know that if I say that God told me something, there is nothing that you can do to change that. When God puts me up on game, it may not make sense to you because most of the time it doesn't even seem sensible to me. But I still believe God and my circle knows that. They know how I feel about God and what He says. Since you have been rocking with me, you know by now too. In fact, when I first started working on this book and tossing around the hashtag **#GPMUOG** in the cybersphere, no one could figure out exactly what it meant but everyone knew at least one of those G's stood for God! Every time I heard that, I smiled. My brand was based on God and I didn't have to tell anyone that. The people could see my messaging clearly.

#GPMUOG – Even if you are not building a business, you are your own personal brand. What are people saying about you? What do you know that you would never budge on? That is branding right there. What people think you believe will determine how people spend their money with you. If you think it's a lie, look at Chick-fil-a. I LOVE me some Chick-fil-a! And I am not here for a debate on how you feel about the controversy. However, the entire LGBT community was ready to shut every single establishment down because of the CEOs stance on gay marriage. People like to spend their money with people who believe what they believe.

FAKE IT 'TIL YOU MAKE IT

My sweet treats business was super tight as a solopreneur that many people didn't even know that I did mostly everything alone. I knew the professional type of image that I wanted for my company. So, if you ever emailed Pizzazzed Plus or talked to Lanie B, then you were corresponding directly with me! Lanie B. was my executive assistant that handled everything concerning Pizzazzed. The Pizzazzed customers adored Lanie because she was the epitome of great customer service! Lanie B. always ended with, "We appreciate your business." I spoke big like I was expecting to be! Often, I received praises on Lanie's character and politeness. "Yes, I know." I would be thinking, "because she is I and I am her!" Lanie worked at Pizzazzed until Pizzazzed could pay my real assistant and I don't regret ever hiring Lanie. The customers always spoke very highly of her/me; however you decide to look at it!

On this journey, you have to sometimes fake it until you make it. I have already mentioned elsewhere that you must exhaust the resources that you have before you can expect to receive more. This includes you as a resource. Unless you are an heiress like Paris (Hilton), you will be working in your business until you can work on your business. The goal is to work yourself out of a job though! Faking it 'til you make it will take you far. But don't forget to FAITH 'til you make it as well!

#GPMUOG – Crazy faith plus hard work always pays off! Clearly, God wants you to get this message before our time is up here. Please don't miss it because I don't want you to miss what He has for you!

Game From

The Struggle

WILLING VESSEL PART ONE

Openly sharing my story is one of those things that His perfect strength empowers me to do. Exposing my vulnerabilities and bearing my nakedness to the world is not an easy feat so I truly need God's help. For the most part, I felt as though I was doing a great job at it, until God spoke and let me know that what I am doing was not nearly enough. "I can't do anything through you my for daughters' benefit, if they don't know what you're going through right now. They have to know how "bad"--and it's really not that bad because I am taking care great of you-- it is because then when I do what I have already told you that I am going to do, their minds can be blown and their faith reinforced. That is how I will win them over. Even in the Bible, every single person who was saved was saved because someone else showed them My power. I am trying to use you girl! All I need is a willing vessel!"

Listen! I typed those exact words as He was telling me! Tears were ferociously leaking from my eyes because I (1) knew what I had to do and (2) I knew God really had His hands on me. If the works of my life could indeed save others' lives, He was going to take great care of me. He loves me so much that He would keep me, but He needed to know that I loved him enough to say "yes" to what He was requiring of me. Once I affirmed, He began to work on me so that I could be used for His purposes. **#GPMUOG** – All God is looking for is a willing vessel. Allow Him to flow freely through you.

Does the Lord delight in burnt offerings and sacrifices as much as in obeying the Lord? To obey is better than sacrifice and to heed is better than the fat of rams. 1 Samuel 15:22 NIV

And he said to them, "The harvest is plentiful, but the laborers are few. Therefore pray earnestly to the Lord of the harvest to send out laborers into his harvest. Luke 10:2 ESV

PAIN IS PAIN

I spend an incredible amount of time on social media because that is one of the places where I have been assigned to spread inspiration and hope. One evening as I was perusing Facebook, I scrolled by a question that piqued my interest. "If you knew that you were going through just to help somebody else, would it make it easier?" I am not usually the person who comments a lot on social media, but I was compelled to add my 24 cents. People – no, not people. Christians. All the Christians on the thread commented a resounding, "Yes, definitely! Because that's what I'm here for." I found it very hard to believe that all those peo– Christians had such a high tolerance for pain that just the thought of helping someone who they may not even know, would make the process less painful. Maybe that was their truth, but I had to speak up for the voiceless who may not be such strong towers in the midst of pain. As a seeker and giver of truth, I had to share mine:

"If I'm honest, no. Pain is pain and it hurts. In the moment, I don't want to go through it for anyone, including myself. However, once I push through it on the other side and have a clear head, I am able to thank God for the lessons learned and the testimony that will help someone else. But while I'm in it, knowing it's for someone else doesn't make it any easier for me. #TruthMoment"

Later, I pondered on additional things that I should've said. You know how it is when you start recounting a verbal disagreement that previously occurred and you think about everything that you could have said to win the argument? Yea, that. Well this is what I would've added: "That doesn't mean that I don't love God. I do. But it still hurts. Jesus was God himself in the flesh but even He hurt. He attempted to pray the most painful burden of the cross away, but He had to go through it to help so many people. **Then he said to them, "My soul is overwhelmed with sorrow to the point of death. Stay here and keep watch with me." Going a little farther, he fell with his face to the ground and prayed, "My Father, if it is possible, may this cup be taken from me. Yet not as I will, but as you will." Matthew 26:38-39 NIV**

That's precisely what was happening in my life when I responded to that status update. I was in excruciating pain. The pressures of trying to build an entrepreneurial empire from scratch, the confusion of not knowing how I truly fit into the world, dealing with a daughter whose attitude was changing for the not-so-better, navigating personal challenges and trying hard to resist the urge of opposition that was trying to pull me back into depression were more than enough to create the very pain that my Facebook "friend" was inquiring about. I knew I wasn't the only one and that's why I had to share my truth. **#GPMUOG** – Just be honest. The more honest you are with people, the more they will trust you. The more they trust you, the more they will connect with you. The more they connect with you, the more they will invest their time and money in you.

THE SCARLET 'F'

As I began to endeavor to truly live my life right before God, premarital sex became one of those pressure points for me. I used to get heavily convicted about having sex when I was unmarried. While it was somewhat of an issue in the relationships of my college days, it was mostly true with my husband before he was my husband. For whatever reason, it was just different with him. I truly desired for our intimate times to be blessed. I wanted it to be sacred. For the most part during our period of dating, we didn't engage. The times when we did give into temptation, we — wait, let me speak for myself – I felt bad. I would roll over and just lie there feeling like I had just committed the worst and most unpardonable sin. The guilt that followed any of our sexual encounters was horrible and it was enough to make me rethink ever doing it again. But

eventually, I always did. There were only a few slip-
ups that I can recall, but regardless of few or many,
there are always consequences for our actions. The
last time that we had sex as an unmarried couple, I
was left lying in the bed with a bit more than the
guilt. A seed had been planted and in 40 weeks I
was going to be welcomed into motherhood. In fact,
I know the exact day I got pregnant. It was the day
he proposed to me. The running joke in my family is
that most people get pregnant on their wedding
night, but we couldn't wait and handled the
business on the day of our engagement!

I can laugh about it now, but back then I thought
I had fallen clean from grace. I was crying day in
and day out. People started calling me Weeping
Wanda! Shame had overtaken me, and I wanted to
run away from my church home because I feared
the judgment that would come from the people
there. The words from one of my dear friends,
Natalie, still ring clearly in my ears. "Who are you
worried about? Those church folks? Girl, bye! They
don't have any room to judge you. Girl, no one is
going to make you wear a scarlet 'F' for fornicator!"
I swear, I am laughing now but there's no doubt
that I was a bawling mess when she was shooting
straight from the hip!

In the early moments of my pregnancy, I really
felt that I had completely let God down and He was
so upset with me. Everyone around me tried to
convince me otherwise to no avail. One friend at the
time told me about her similar ordeal. She had
gotten pregnant twice out of wedlock and felt the
judgment of "those church folks" but she reassured

me that she made it through and I would too. While I appreciated her efforts to console me, along with the efforts of so many others, I was still living under a spirit of condemnation. So many people were speaking to me, but it wasn't until God spoke that I was completely free and able to enjoy the beauty of the blessing that I had been chosen to carry. **#GPMUOG** – All it takes is one word from Him to change your situation! I was blessed enough to receive several more words! "Your baby is not the sin. Only I can bless you with a baby and I have given you a divine and perfect gift. Even through your sinful act, I blessed you."

How gracious and thoughtful He is towards us! If you are struggling right now with the fact that you are pregnant (or anything else that you are allowing to hold you back), let that go girl. Ask God to forgive you for the sinful act and get to loving on your baby. He/she needs you! My first born, Karizma, is truly a blessing to me. She's a blessing to our entire family. Her prayers rout demons from our home. Karizma means, "a gift granted by the Holy Spirit for the good of the church." That means that she's also a blessing to the entire kingdom of God. God indeed blessed us, but I wouldn't even be able to appreciate the blessings if I was still a hostage living behind satan's bars of guilt, shame and condemnation.

LOAN SHARKS

My policy is very simple when it comes to

loaning money to people. I don't! **#GPMUOG** – If you cannot afford to simply give what is being requested, then you cannot afford to loan it either. That way, if you don't get the money back, you don't have to feel like the relationship is over and your finances are not negatively affected because you were never expecting it back anyway. Likewise, most times when your friends and family ask you for a loan, they can't truly afford to pay you back either. This is not to say that you will never receive your money back, but every dime that comes through their hands is now obligated to you until their debt is paid. That is why the Bible says that the borrower is a slave to the lender. (**Proverbs 22:7**) If you must be the lender, I encourage you to never loan money to people who aren't loyal to you. They will break their necks not to pay you back. But somebody that is loyal will break themselves just to uphold their commitment to reimburse you. The loyal friend will skip paying a bill and any other priorities that they have, to pay you because they wouldn't dare jeopardize your relationship over some money. I learned those lessons the hard way, by loaning money that I couldn't afford to people who couldn't afford to pay me back and by borrowing money that I didn't have room to reimburse. God put me up on that good game through tough lessons, lost money, and broken relationships.

VALLEY TIME IS CRUCIAL TO YOUR GROWTH

The "valley" is a figurative location where we go when life is happening in a bad way. The sponsor of our trip to the valley can be an ended relationship, failing health, limited finances, problems at work, wayward children, and the list goes on and on. Our valley trip sponsors are not always the same, but the constant for us all is that being in the valley is painful. No one willingly and excitedly raises their hand to spend time in the valley. I don't know too many people who are volunteering to take a trip to the lowest of lows of life. After all, it is lonely, cold and sometimes even very depressing down in the valley. Thus, most people run at the first indication that valley time is near. Unfortunately for them, there is no way out of spending time in the valley. In fact, it is extremely crucial to your growth as a player. You need the valley to garner all the good game!

You do not learn game when you are standing on the mountain peak. Nope. You are privy to the most essential information when you have a temporary tent pitched in your valley. You can hear God's voice clearly in your temporary residence because you don't have the noise and distractions that go on up top. In 2015, when I was spending what I thought was way too much time in the valley, I cried out and asked God why was I checked in the Extended Stay Valley. I was convinced that I had long overstayed my welcome! The analogy that He gave me that day blew my mind. If you were going on a real trip on an airplane, the flight attendants would start giving you all the most important information such as emergency plans and the location of the lavatories before you even start to ascend into the clouds. 1) It is important that you have the information before you start getting distracted with sleep, movies, chatting with your seat neighbor or finishing some work on your laptop. 2) You can hear the instructions much better on the ground. The sounds of propellers, engines, wind and so much more can create major competition and impede you from getting the necessary information for a safe and successful flight. If you are anything like me, then you have major ear problems anytime you take a flight. Mine are usually so stopped up that I cannot hear anything. All sounds around me are muffled. **#GPMUOG –** Don't run from your valley time. Instead, reside there gracefully knowing that God only has you there because there is information that you must learn for your journey.

THERE'S BEAUTY IN THE STRUGGLE

Everyone wants to tell you how to get rich and I thoroughly appreciate some good information on how to add some coinage to my piggy bank and some stacks under my mattress. I think it's equally important, though, to share with you how to make it while you're in those lack days because those are the moments that will expose how strong (or weak) you really are. ***Don't be sleeping on your level 'cause it's beauty in the struggle... (J. Cole, Love Yourz)*** As you are building the life, you will probably land in moments of time where what you have is not what you are accustomed to having. You just may find yourself there a time or two during this life and I don't want you plunging from the 47th floor of your high rise because you couldn't withstand the pressure. If you are not in a lack season of your life today, I earnestly pray that it remains that way. However, if you find yourself struggling to make ends meet, I want to encourage you during this process. I also pray for you that this will be the last time that you find yourself with these circumstances. I once heard a powerful woman, Tonie Robinson, speak this affirmation: "I will never be broke again."

#GPMUOG – The first order of business when you are struggling is to envision yourself not struggling. Not only do you have to see it before it manifests, you need to speak it. The Word of God declares that no good thing would God withhold from you. **(Psalm 84:11)** God also promised to bring you wealth. **(Proverbs 10:22)** *Say what you heard so you can see what said. (Israel Houghton, No Limits)*

While you are working through your "in between blessings" period, you will probably find it challenging to make unnecessary necessary purchases. No, that's not a typo. An oxymoron, yes, but not a typo because I emphatically meant both of those words. Unnecessary but still necessary. You know those new clothes that you would love to purchase but can't really afford but you need because as a new business owner you must make an appearance at social events. That's an unnecessary

necessary purchase. If you are practicing responsible adulting, then you go back and forth about whether you absolutely need it. Sometimes the unnecessary need is victorious; other times it takes a backseat to an absolute necessity like groceries. But on the rare days that you choose those oxymoron purchases, you still have to be responsible.

#GPMUOG – Buy timeless pieces that can be interchanged for various outfits. Leave the trendy and flashy options for special occasions or when you can afford to spend money on an outfit that you can only wear once a year. My girls would swear that I went shopping every time I had to go somewhere but I would always joke that it was simply because I was gifted with the ability to dress. My closet was scarcely full (yep, another oxymoron) of about twelve pieces. From those dozens of items, I could put together at least 28 ½ outfits. More than likely, I needed another shirt to tip over to 29!

I have never been one of those people to completely eradicate my social and entertainment life when I was dealing with a financial storm. That simply was not an option for me. After all, you need self-care to sustain, especially when you are going through difficult times in your life. The key is to find free to very low-cost activities to indulge in.

#GPMOUG – You can still have fun when your money is funny. There are so many exciting and unique activities that you can participate in for free.99! All you have to do is google, "things to do in my city for free.99." Okay, fine! Take the .99 off, but if you are looking to attend all the urban events then leave it on. Pause. I had to chuckle on that one! Seriously, don't feel guilty about stepping out every now and then to enjoy yourself. Moderation is the $20 buzzword.

When I was low on cash, I tried my hardest to ensure that my children were not affected by my misfortunes. Like most parents who pride themselves on being great parents, I always made it happen for my babies. Scraping up money and creating experiences for my girls was a no-brainer. Many times, they didn't even cost because, as you should know by now, I am the queen of a good free.99 deal!

#GPMUOG – Choose experiences over things. It is imperative that you create the spaces for your children to experience life. Please don't let money become an insurmountable obstacle and reason why you cannot curate various experiences in their lives, and, don't succumb to the "I don't have time" syndrome. You would be so surprised at how easy it is to please them. They usually don't require a lot of money to be spent; they just want quality time well spent.

#GPMUOG – Take care of what God has already blessed you with. "Team iPhone" is what I have been screaming since The Man purchased my very first iPhone 4 one Mother's Day. I don't have time to argue with you delusional Android users and honestly, it is not even that I am uber loyal to the Apple brand. It's just that the learning curve frightens me; I just don't have the energy to learn how to do use anything else. So, Team iPhone it is!

Any of my fellow teammates can attest to how

ridiculously fragile those darn phones are. One wrong landing and the entire face is completely shattered. Such was the case for me. If you have ever had to walk around with a raggedy phone, then you know firsthand how embarrassing it is. You don't want to pull out your phone to take pictures, which is difficult for me because I am Picture Patty. You barely want to get on it when people call. God forbid there is an emergency that requires our attention. We will leave the phone in our purses and make sure the volume is up to hear the speakerphone conversation. The whole scene is utterly ridiculous. Yet, we do what we can to save face. Imagine how I felt having to do all of that and some for several months on end. After speaking to Apple, who was the only place that I trusted to service my device, I learned that it would cost $129 to repair my screen. As ugly as that little iPhone was, I decided that wasn't a cost that I was ready to eat. Instead, I spent that money on getting me closer to my destiny. It may not have been much, but it was something that could catapult me from where I was standing. Shoot, I probably needed that money to pay my cell phone bill. I needed to be able to connect with people for opportunities.

#GPMUOG – When funds are low and when funds are plentiful, be selective with how you spend your money. If it doesn't make you, your family or your situation better, chances are that purchase can wait. Eventually, I was relieved to take my phone into Apple for repair, but it was only after the damage started affecting the functionality of the phone. I don't think I was ever that happy to spend

$130!

"Ignorance is the most expensive thing on the planet." I first heard The Biological's father share that quote. Yes, technically, I am referring to my grandfather but I'm almost certain that I have never used that terminology before this very moment to describe him. Those may be the only words that he has spoken that I have held onto. When you really ponder on those nine words, you realize just how powerful they are. What you do not know can cost you money, time, opportunities, and even relationships. I found that quote particularly relevant during the season of my life when it was difficult to do all the things that I was accustomed to when my civil engineer checks were flowing on a bi-weekly basis. Maintaining things like my hair, nails, skin, and other beauty treatments were most times out of my monthly budget, but they still had to be taken care of. So, I went to YouTube University! I learned how to do everything that I couldn't exactly afford to pay for.

#GPMUOG – Humble yourself and learn how to take care of yourself. Do what you have to do until you don't have to do it anymore. Work yourself out of a job! I was determined to fire me as the hair stylist, nail technician, and esthetician so I worked that much harder!

#GPUMOG – Your process and journey to what God has deemed success for your life may not look even remotely similar to your neighbor's. Your life may be littered with struggles, chaos, and detours, but trust that if you are being obedient to what He has called you to do, then He has you right where

He wants you to be. God has some of that good game that He wants to share with you during this season of your life. Seasons change! Don't get entangled in anyone else's lane, trying to live their life. Simply Love Yourz!

SUCCESS IS IN THE STRETCHING

As God was stretching me in preparation for my next season, He started asking me to do some things that were far beyond the limits of my comfort zone. I vividly remember Him making me call a young lady to the carpet about how she was operating her business. At first, I tried to reason with God. "Why should I have to tell her that? She is not even my friend?" Let me warn you; don't ask Him a question if you are not prepared to hear the hard truth! He checked me so fast! "Because you love to empower Black women so much. Yet, you are going to sit back and watch a young sister sabotage what she is trying to build?"

"...that they [older women] admonish the young women to love their husbands, to love their children, to be discreet, chaste, homemakers, good, obedient to their own husbands, that the word of God may not be blasphemed." Titus 2:4-5 NKJV

He went on to tell me that if I was willing to do everything that He was instructing me to do, He was going to elevate me. **#GPMUOG** – When you are growing and elevating, God is going to require you to do some hard things that you may not want to do. He needs to see if you are truly obedient and there are some areas that you can only grow in by being uncomfortable. Growth seldom comes from experiences that make you feel good.

I had no desire to call that girl and relay the information that God was urging me to because I felt in my spirit that it was not going to be well received. I called her anyway and I was absolutely right. The conversation began with upbeat chatter but once I started bearing the bad news, her temperament quickly shifted. However, the more I shared what I had been sent to deliver, the easier I found it to complete my assignment and ultimately pass my test. **#GPMUOG** – Whenever you are standing on the brink of elevation, God will send a series of tests to see if you will obey Him. Your next level will only come with the passing of those exams. I am generous and want to see you win so I will share this cheat sheet with you -- the test only has one right answer and that is yes! All he needs is your yes to whatever He is requesting of you...and of course your actions to validate that yes. Remember the two of the most important pieces of game? If not, go back to Game 101 and refresh your memory!

Listen! Obedience is better than sacrifice. 1 Samuel 15:22 NLT

THE POINT IS TO PUSH PAST THE PAIN

I know we all hit bad times at some point. But the point is pushing past that pain. Man, if I could make you understand how broke I was at the end of 2015 and the beginning of 2016. *I originally wrote that last line at the beginning of 2016. I am sitting here on December 23, 2016 and penning this addendum. I am STILL broke. Don't put a deadline on God's timing! (Unless He gives you an actual date.)* During the last quarter of 2015 I slipped into a serious depression. I would wake up crying and stain the same pillows with tears as I forced myself to sleep at night. My dear husband had no idea how to support me, but he did an amazing job doing it! I thank God for him too. Heck, I didn't even know what I needed at that time in my life so for him to really hold me up meant the world. I am sure I have probably already said this, but I truly praise God for giving me that man for where I was going not for where I was. Like man, God, You are so freaking amazing! In Your divine wisdom, You knew I would hit the roughest patch of my journey at almost 35 years old, but You had predestined my future and my helpmeet to assist me through that turmoil. You gave me the necessity for where You were about to launch me. You have to realize how dope it is that He loves You that much. **#GPMUOG** -- He is not just supplying your needs, He has already supplied your needs before the need ever arises. That's Atlantic Ocean, launch out deep right there!

Anyway, back to the story. We were broke. Very broke. I had been working my sweet treats company, Pizzazzed Plus, but for whatever reason, my clientele had drastically declined. So, it was just hard. When income tax season rolled around, I was determined to put myself in a much better position. Honey, I was strategic! My Clutch Girl, who is also my tax lady, worked hard to get me every single cent owed to me. When that direct deposit hit, I didn't ball out of control with that money. There were no 60" screens, no Victoria's Secret Pink splurges, no luxury car purchases with $5,000 down payments, none of that! Why, you ask? Well for one, I think that is just downright stupid! Sorry, not sorry! I can call it stupid because I have done it before. But two, because if I would've balled out like that I would have been right back in the same situation 5 months later. Ladies, when you get a lump sum of money like that, stop running out spending it like you have never had anything. Instead, invest in yourself! And that's what I did. As soon as that check hit my account, I started putting the wheels in motion for *I'm The One That Got Away*. As a matter of fact, the wheels had already been in motion. I was anticipating my income tax refund and when it arrived late February, I already had all my preparations on standby. By March 15th, I had launched my new movement. I was selling t-shirts, bags, mugs, and empowering women to be everything God had created them to be through blogs, talks, and by sharing my platform with other women who had stories of being the one that got away. *I'm The One That Got Away* was born from an idea from God, just like every other thing that I couldn't have dreamt on my own. I was just in my bed one day and it clicked. I had been telling women for years to be the one that got away whenever I would be consoling them from a breakup. So that night in the bed, I got to thinking about all the guys who had once told me that I was the one that got away.

That's when it was born! Just like that. I went to share with The Man and he said, "Man that's cold, Krissi." My nickname is purposely misspelled because that's how he spells it. Neither of the two most important men in my life know how to spell my name. My Daddy spells it Krissey and then The Man spells it Krissi. The latter used to irritate me so because I was constantly correcting his spelling, yet he never really seemed to grasp the concept. One day I just decided to drop it and move on. If that is how he chose to spell my name, then I accepted it as him creating his own unique way to describe his wife. **#GPMUOG** – Learn how to see the light in things. Stop focusing on the glass being half empty and thank God for the half glass of juice to quench your thirst on a hot summer day!

So, back to The Man. He went on to say, "You have to do something with that." I had zero inkling as to what I was really doing, but what I did know was that I was never returning to the dark and twisted place that God had just delivered me from.

Okay, so you are probably thinking, "Girl, you just said that you were still broke at the beginning of 2017 too!" Yes, you caught me. But you also know by now that I won't lie to you. At the top of 2017, I was still trying to figure out who I loved more, Peter or Paul. – Someone will start a malicious rumor about me having an affair with two different men, but the clever ones already caught that. – The difference in 2017, which coincidentally is the year that I wrote this exact line, is that I may have been broke but my spirit was not broken. Hopefully, I find the energy to dive into that in a later chapter.

SEX IS BETTER WHEN THE BILLS ARE PAID

Look, you already know how I feel about sex as it seems like every other chapter I am bringing up the word. However, this one isn't even really about that; I just wanted to get your attention. Now that I got it, listen closely, please!

Being financially strapped can cause a lot of strain on any relationship and mine was no different. When The Man and I found ourselves waist deep in debt after an unexpected employment loss, we initially battled each other. That had to be one of the stupidest mistakes that we have ever made during our marriage. **#GPMUOG** – When teammates turn on each other, there is absolutely no way that team can win. You do understand that you and your spouse are teammates, right? Did you just say no? Okay, you need to press pause on this book for a while and go find Marriage 101. God Put Me up on Game is a 300 level class and assumes that you've already completed the prerequisite coursework. So, go play catch up! I promise to be right here waiting for you when you get back.

Anywho, things between The Man and I got really bad and I am ashamed to admit that I acted a plum fool. Wait. What is a plum fool anyway? Is it worse than a peach fool or an apple fool? Sorry, but inquiring minds want to know! Well, maybe I acted somewhere between a peach and a plum fool, but whichever it was, I was so ugly. I spoke some things out of my mouth that I almost immediately regretted. But now I look back and I'm wondering why I was acting such a fool. Knowing what God had already told me concerning our financial situation should have been enough for me to hold my peace and not fall right into one of satan's attacks. God had previously revealed that He was going to bless us so abundantly, but He had to ensure that any cracks in our marriage were sealed beforehand. That way having money or prestige could never tear us apart. Honey, if you think that you are having problems inside of your marriage being broke, try adding seven zeros to your account balances. People act a banana fool when they get their hands on some money, especially when they have never had any. *Acting like a n***a who ain't never had... (Juvenile, Rich N****z)* God didn't want us acting like those people who Juvie was rapping about. **#GPMUOG** – If He has already told you that everything is going to be okay, then why are you stressing during the storm? It's either because you don't believe the revelation or human nature is just pushing you to be afraid.

That valley time of our finances was to force us to learn how to make it together. Yes, we could have easily walked away from each other when things got rough. But no. We needed each other. We had to stay together. We were better together. *I'm a movement by myself, but I'm a force when we're together... (Fabolous featuring Ne-Yo, Make Me Better)* And neither of us would've left the other one in the state we were in. Anyone who has ever cared anything about you won't leave you while you are down. So, I fought hard for my marriage when the external issues were fighting even harder. I was not about to let my marriage fall apart over something as dispensable as money. We made a vow to cleave to one another through richer or poorer. We couldn't let go because we hadn't made it to our richer part yet! **#GPMUOG** – Don't let pressure make you give up right before it's about to get good!

Yes, I have heard that sex feels better when the bills are paid, but I am a living witness that it can also feel great when they're almost, barely, or "I need to make an arrangement" paid. You just have to be willing to commit to your spouse as you both commit to working through your season of lack together.

GREEN-EYED MONSTER

Going through your own personal hell while watching people around you flourish in every area of their life is an almost inexplicable kind of hard. It is especially hard to witness if you have allowed your own circumstances to stagnate you. During the most horrific year of my life, I could not stand to watch anyone excel at anything. In 2015, I was in buried in a deep abyss of depression. An array of events triggered my depression and contributed to how I felt during those dark moments, but the main issue was that I didn't feel as though I was where I was supposed to be in life. Unsuccessful, failure, and embarrassment were all words that I used to label myself. Beating my 35-year-old self up about not being further along on my journey ultimately morphed into me not being able to celebrate anyone else who had reached or surpassed that figurative benchmark of success. Social media surely didn't make my life any easier. While I was basking in my misery, I was watching women who look like me do things that I wanted to do with my family and in my business. For the first real time in life, I found myself envious of women winning. I mean I was mad at celebrities for getting married and I had a great husband at home. I was pissed at social media "friends" who were inking business deals and I had just moved my dessert business into a storefront.

As if being depressed wasn't enough, I had become a hater and that is no claim to fame that I ever care to adopt. I am Taraji's little sister. I exude support for my sisters. I stop what I am doing, stand up and do the slow clap whenever I see one of them winning. A come-up for one of us is a come-up for all of us. "I'm happy when black women win; the significant is important to the whole." When I read those words in *Around the Way Girl*, I couldn't have agreed more. Honey, I put my book down, proudly stood up and looked west towards Hollywood to return Taraji's slow clap right back to her. Now that I think of it, I probably should have turned to the north towards the city of Chicago because she was probably in town filming Empire. But I digress.

I honestly get bubbly inside when women make strides in every facet of their lives. I love to see us killing it as wives, mothers, daughters, sisters, friends, career women, entrepreneurs, ministers, philanthropists, entertainers, Wal-Mart greeters, whatever! So, imagine how I felt when I realized that I had become the green-eyed monster! I went straight to God because I needed His help.

#GPMUOG – Don't settle for being something or someone that you know you are not. The enemy will try to use your circumstances to make you into a negative person. Often, you may be so broken that you alone cannot suppress the urges to become that person. The good news is that you don't have to. Allow God to help you!

Per usual, He came through and helped a sistah out! Thank God that it was quick too; I couldn't stand to be that chick for too long. He immediately showed me the root cause of my jealousy and where I was failing. I was finding it toilsome to praise the strides of my peers simply because I hadn't arrived where they were. I was struggling with the thought of saluting their noteworthy accomplishments because I was not doing a damn thing to change my own situation. Did I ever mention that I cuss just a little? Every now and then I have to use a not-so-bad word for emphasis. I don't do it much and I never use those harsh ones…unless it's The Man and me having our own private fun, but that's an entirely different story.

#GPMUOG – The only people who are mad at someone else's gains are the ones who are doing nothing to recover from their own losses. If you are sitting around just watching other people make major moves, you will always be mad when they hit significant milestones. However, if you are busy running your own race, you won't have the time nor energy to consume yourself with how far ahead someone else is. Her successes will become a source of inspiration for you and not a point of contention. You will be completing your marathon at your pace, celebrating yourself along the journey and every now and then you will peek over and see your girl winning. Pause on your track, give her a nice, Taraji slow clap and then get back to work!

The most interesting thing about the green-eyed monster is that we are usually coveting someone's success and there is another young lady somewhere watching us and doing the exact same thing. Of course, in our moments of doubt and despair, we never understand why anyone would want the pains, struggles, and mishaps of our lives. Well, those are the same thoughts of that woman whose life we are seeking. Why? Because we all wear our best moments like a badge of honor on our sleeves. However, it's those moments of pain, lack, and defeat that really shape us into the women that we are today. So, if you want her life or the next one is secretly wishing for yours, I hope both of you are ready for the warfare that comes along with the win!

Kristen R. Harris

Game From

The Blessed

146

THE MARK OF THE BLESSED

On September 14, 2017, I sat in my bathroom gazing at my lavender bathroom wall while the rest of my family peacefully slumbered. I was full of goosebumps because I was sitting on the toilet with no clothes on. Don't worry, I wasn't using the bathroom or taking care of my business as my mother-in-law says! Well, now that I think about, I was, in fact, taking care of business. My bathroom had become an unorthodox office at 12:13 in the morning. My red robe or housecoat, as my Grandma would say, was strewn on the floor just barely covering my right pinky toe. My laptop was resting on my shivering knees all for the sake of making this reading moment possible for you. A quick glance to the left revealed my new desk for the next several minutes. In actuality, it was just the vanity and I had to be extra careful not to tip my belongings over into the damp sink. I had already been sitting there about 45 minutes scribbling notes in my red composition book when I realized that I needed to grab my laptop and phone charger and return to my makeshift office. For whatever reason, my lavender lavatory was where God had called this late night/early morning meeting.

The hour or so that I spent perched on the toilet helped me to put some major things into perspective. I gained clarity on many things that I had been praying about. God revealed the areas where I was falling short and the things that I was doing to personally sabotage my blessings. As I reflect now, I wonder if my nakedness was symbolic of me being completely stripped before the Lord. There was no hiding or covering up in that meeting. **#GPMUOG** – "Be open to receiving from Me anywhere, at any time. Don't try to put Me in a box. I am omnipresent and speak and perform miracles wherever I please."

Perhaps the most impactful encounter that night happened just as I assumed that our meeting had concluded. My fingers were no longer pecking away at my keyboard, so it seemed as if the Boss was done speaking with me. Just as I was closing my laptop and gathering my robe from the floor, I noticed 3 numbers on the lavender wall. The marking wasn't from a writing utensil, so I couldn't blame my 5-year-old Kai Pie. It wasn't even a carving or etching so I couldn't chastise her older sisters either. Instead, it appeared as if the paint on the wall has been mysteriously raised to form the three numbers: 7-7-7.

The greatest sense of peace overtook me in that moment. It was as if God was saying, "If 6-6-6 is the mark of the beast, then know that 7-7-7 is the mark of the BLESSED." In case you didn't know, the number 7 represents spiritual perfection and completion. The writing was literally on the wall! Everything that we had just discussed in our meeting would be perfected and completed.

And I am sure of this, that he who began a good work in you will bring it to completion at the day of Jesus Christ. Philippians 1:6 ESV

THANK YOU MAKES ROOM FOR MORE

My social media "friends" will attest to the fact that I try to like and thank every single person who comments on my page. I am just of the mindset that if you took time out of your day to stop by my page and say something, then I want to at least acknowledge that. I don't take anyone's kindness for granted. My Sissy thinks that I am a serial lunatic for doing this. However, I do it now because I recognize that one day I won't be able to respond to every single message. Honestly speaking, and not being cocky, I have always known that I was destined for greatness and was going to be someone major. Maybe you may have just found out with this book. But if I let you know today how much I sincerely appreciate you, then I don't have to stress about you knowing it when it becomes impossible to respond.

One of the ways that you can ensure that you remain humble is to always say thank you. Thank you to God. Thank you to people. The only people who don't say thank you regard themselves much higher than they ought. They think they've done everything on their own and don't need to acknowledge anyone. When the reality is, everything that we have been given is by the grace and selflessness of God for His purposes. You are not just smart to be a smart girl. He has need of that. You are not just pretty to be a pretty face. No, God knew that the world paralleled beauty and influence and He needed to use that influence. Remember to remain humble! **#GPMUOG** – Thank you makes room for more. So, thank you God, for this gift! Thank YOU for making it this far in my book! You are the real MVP!

Game Doesn't Die

A WILLING VESSEL PART TWO

To know that God has chosen to use me is mind-blowing. God, who alone is God and doesn't need anyone to help Him accomplish what He wants to accomplish, sought me out. He's using me because I'm willing to be used. All He needs is a willing vessel! I'm special to God as His daughter, but I'm not special in a way that anyone else can't be used as well. No, He can use you and all the pieces of your life if you're just willing to be used. **#GPMUOG** – All He wants is a yes! Yield to His way and watch Him change your life.

THE GAME DOESN'T DIE

I just used almost 40,000 words spilling out my truth and putting you up on that good, good game. For that reason, I really don't feel like adding anything else to wrap this thing up! Don't judge me! But I will share this one last thought. I have a multitude of other experiences that schooled me to the game. Those experiences taught me lessons about love, friendships, prayer, persistence and so much more. I can't wait to huddle up with you again to share it with you. Life will have taken me on some new turns by then and I will have that fresh game for you too! Stay tuned. **#GPUMOG** – "As long as you are living your life and are open to receive, I will always be here to put you on game." In the meantime, take all the game from this one and play the heck out of life so it doesn't play you! Kristen R. Harris, girl of the far Southside and I'm out! *drops mic in the best "Obama out" fashion*

Sharer of the Game

Kristen R. Harris subscribes to the notion that every woman is full of potential and purpose but many lack the knowledge on how to get everything out that is inside of them. Kristen helps draw it out by equipping them with the tools they need to get unstuck. As a Spiritual Midwife, Kristen helps women realize that they are pregnant with purpose and push past their pain to deliver everything that God has promised them. Her books, *EmpowerMoments for the Everyday Mom* and *EmpowerMoments for the Everyday Woman* and *Queens Turn Pain Into Power* and more have positively impacted women's lives around the globe. Outside of writing, Kristen's vibrant smile comes from The Man and her 3 Piece Spicy.

66241877R00096